VIOLENCE AND SPORTS
DANGEROUS GAMES

By Tyler Stevenson

Portions of this book originally appeared in *Sports Violence* by Anne Wallace Sharp.

D1709802

LUCENT
P R E S S

Published in 2020 by
Lucent Press, an Imprint of Greenhaven Publishing, LLC
353 3rd Avenue
Suite 255
New York, NY 10010

Copyright © 2020 Greenhaven Press, a part of Gale, Cengage Learning
Gale and Greenhaven Press are registered trademarks used herein under license.

All new materials copyright © 2020 Lucent Press, an Imprint of Greenhaven Publishing, LLC.

All rights reserved. No part of this book may be reproduced in any form without permission
in writing from the publisher, except by a reviewer.

Designer: Deanna Paternostro
Editor: Jennifer Lombardo

Cataloging-in-Publication Data

Names: Stevenson, Tyler.
Title: Violence and sports: dangerous games /Tyler Stevenson.
Description: New York : Lucent Press, 2020. | Series: Hot topics | Includes index.
Identifiers: ISBN 9781534568136 (pbk.) | ISBN 9781534568143 (library bound) | ISBN
9781534568150 (ebook)
Subjects: LCSH: Violence in sports–Juvenile literature. | Sports–Sociological aspects–Juvenile
literature.
Classification: LCC GV706.7 S534 2020 | DDC 796–dc23

Printed in China

Some of the images in this book illustrate individuals who are models. The depictions do
not imply actual situations or events

CPSIA compliance information: Batch #BW20KL: For further information contact Greenhaven Publishing LLC, New York,
New York at 1-844-317-7404.

Please visit our website, www.greenhavenpublishing.com. For a free color catalog of all our
high-quality books, call toll free 1-844-317-7404 or fax 1-844-317-7405.

Maywood Public Library
459 Maywood Avenue
Maywood, NJ 07607
(201)845-2915

CONTENTS

FOREWORD 4

INTRODUCTION 6
Violence Around the World

CHAPTER 1 10
What Is Allowed?

CHAPTER 2 31
Violence and Competition

CHAPTER 3 46
Violence Off the Field

CHAPTER 4 56
Spectator Violence

CHAPTER 5 72
How Can Violence in Sports Be Prevented?

NOTES 88

DISCUSSION QUESTIONS 94

ORGANIZATIONS TO CONTACT 96

FOR MORE INFORMATION 98

INDEX 100

PICTURE CREDITS 103

ABOUT THE AUTHOR 104

Adolescence is a time when many people begin to take notice of the world around them. News channels, blogs, and talk radio shows are constantly promoting one view or another; very few are unbiased. Young people also hear conflicting information from parents, friends, teachers, and acquaintances. Often, they will hear only one side of an issue or be given flawed information. People who are trying to support a particular viewpoint may cite inaccurate facts and statistics on their blogs, and news programs present many conflicting views of important issues in our society. In a world where it seems everyone has a platform to share their thoughts, it can be difficult to find unbiased, accurate information about important issues.

It is not only facts that are important. In blog posts, in comments on online videos, and on talk shows, people will share opinions that are not necessarily true or false, but can still have a strong impact. For example, many young people struggle with their body image. Seeing or hearing negative comments about particular body types online can have a huge effect on the way someone views himself or herself and may lead to depression and anxiety. Although it is important not to keep information hidden from young people under the guise of protecting them, it is equally important to offer encouragement on issues that affect their mental health.

The titles in the Hot Topics series provide readers with different viewpoints on important issues in today's society. Many of these issues, such as students' rights, are of immediate concern to young people. This series aims to give readers factual context on these crucial topics in a way that lets them form their own opinions. The facts presented throughout also serve to empower readers to help themselves or support people they know who are struggling with many of the challenges adolescents face today. Although negative viewpoints are not ignored or downplayed, this series allows young people to see that the challenges they face are not insurmountable. As increasing numbers of young adults join public debates, especially regarding their own rights, learning the facts as well as the views of others will help them decide where they stand—and understand what they are fighting for.

Quotes encompassing all viewpoints are presented and cited so readers can trace them back to their original source, verifying for themselves whether the information comes from a reputable place. Additional books and websites are listed, giving readers a starting point from which to continue their own research. Chapter questions encourage discussion, allowing young people to hear and understand their classmates' points of view as they further solidify their own. Full-color photographs and enlightening charts provide a deeper understanding of the topics at hand. All of these features augment the informative text, helping young people understand the world they live in and formulate their own opinions concerning the best way they can improve it.

Violence Around the World

Many people have made the argument that violence is a natural human trait. Since the beginning of human evolution, civilizations all over the world have had to deal with violence of one type or another. Wars, riots, and violent takeovers of governments showcase violence on a large scale, but violence occurs every day on a small scale as well.

Violence has also long had a major role in popular entertainment throughout human history. In addition to TV shows, movies, comic books, and video games, violence has always been present in the world of sports. Sometimes, as in sports such as boxing and wrestling, the violence is the point of the entire competition: People watch to see who can inflict the most damage on the other contender. In other sports, including basketball,

In some sports, such as boxing, violence is the entire point.

football, and soccer, violent acts take place to help the players achieve other goals, such as scoring a point or stopping their opponent from doing so. Linemen in football hurl their bodies at each other to open lanes for running backs to dart through; basketball players meet each other in midair at the rim—one trying to put the ball through the hoop, the other trying to use their body to block the shot. Although violence has historically had a place in sports, some people have expressed concern that the amount and frequency of the violence has been increasing in recent years and has had a negative effect on both players and fans. Researcher Dawn Comstock of Ohio State University explained in 2006, "Our ... research studies have shown sports related violence appears to exist across the board in all sports and seems to be increasing."[1]

Understanding Violence

Violence is defined as the use of physical force to injure, abuse, damage, or destroy. There is some ambiguity as to what constitutes a violent play on the field, but most observers are of the opinion that they recognize it when they see it. In general, an action is considered violent when it occurs outside the rules. However, there are many actions within the rules of sports that end in pain or injury for the players. Outside of the immediate impact, sports violence can have long-lasting, permanent implications for athletes.

Violence is viewed very differently in the context of a sport than it is in everyday life. Tackling someone and driving them to the ground on the sidewalk, for example, is illegal and would likely result in assault charges, but the same act on the football field would be praised as a tough, hard-nosed play even if it resulted in injury to the opposing player. Writer Jay Coakley explained, "Athletes are often praised for their extreme actions that risk health and well-being and inflict pain and injury on others, whereas non-athletes would be defined as deviant for doing the same things."[2]

Athletes are praised and looked up to for their ability to use their bodies—to take a hit and keep going or to hit someone else and slow them down. People watching football like to see hard hits in the open field, and such plays are often shown on highlight reels after the game is over. Professional athletes are often much larger and stronger than the average person, so the hits and collisions are also larger and more physical. Social psychologist Gordon W. Russell suggested, "Outside of wartime, sport is perhaps the only setting in which acts of interpersonal aggression are not only tolerated but enthusiastically applauded by large segments in society. It is interesting to consider that if the mayhem of the [boxing] ring or gridiron [football field] were to erupt in a shopping mall, criminal charges would inevitably follow."[3]

Despite the permanent damage that sports violence can cause to the players, the spectacle of a professional sporting event remains a basic part of many countries' identities. As U.S. president Bill Clinton said in 1998, "America is a sports crazy country, and we often see games as a ... symbol of what we are as a people."[4] Clinton, along with many other Americans, felt that sports reflected all the positive attributes of a society, such as hard work and competition. Like a propensity for violence, this view is not unique to America. A common feeling among many people around the world is that participation in sports should be a rite of passage for young men and women because playing sports builds character and teaches children the importance of sacrifice and teamwork. However, other people disagree with this opinion. Writer Viv Saunders noted that on the opposite side of the issue, "Some believe sport represents all that ... [is] bad in the American character—excessive greed, commercialism, violence, drug abuse, and cheating."[5]

Authors Lynn Jamieson and Thomas Orr argue that, either way, sports help reveal the values of a nation and its citizens. They wrote,

> Sports is merely a reflection of society, one lens by which we define what that society stands for and creates as an image for itself ... It is a positive reflection, for the most part, but the phenomena that surround the violent aspects of sports reveal a great deal of the underbelly of a society's character, and herein, reflect on all of those who participate either directly or indirectly in the sport experience.[6]

Violence is frequently present at varying levels of severity in every level of athletics and every type of sport, from preschool soccer teams all the way up to the highest levels of Olympic competition. In addition to existing on the playing field, violence is also present in the stands. Fans throw things on the field and heckle, or verbally abuse, participants. Opposing fans, some of whom are under the influence of alcohol, fight each other in the stands and yell abuse at referees and officials. Violence in sports can be self-inflicted as well, including injuries resulting from performance-enhancing drug use and "playing through it," which defines the idea that an athlete should push themselves to continue to perform when injured rather than letting their body heal. Within the realm of sports, many people consider this a sign of strength and willpower, but it can cause permanent damage to a person's body. Athletes are encouraged to win at all costs, often at the expense of their bodies and minds, so they can entertain spectators and not let down their teammates. The difficulty in addressing sports violence revolves around the issue of defining what is acceptable or unacceptable during a game.

The spectacle of a professional sporting event is a huge part of a country's identity. Shown here are fans cheering on the Portuguese women's futsal (a variation of soccer) team at a match between Portugal and Bolivia.

CHAPTER 1

What Is Allowed?

Most sports have rules that govern which types of violence are acceptable and which are not. For some sports—such as gymnastics, where team members compete one at a time—this type of rule is not necessary. In other sports, such as hockey or soccer, it is expected that players will shove each other out of the way, but some actions are considered to be unfair.

Most experts agree that there are two kinds of sports violence—sanctioned and unsanctioned, or within the rules and against the rules. Many sports, they explain, such as ice hockey and boxing, are violent by their very nature. Contact, rough play, and even punching are considered normal parts of those sports. While most sports experts consider these acts acceptable, there is also a growing group of sociologists and psychologists who believe that even this normally accepted violence is unjustified and unhealthy.

Some sports experts define sports violence only as a malicious, or purposely harmful, act by a player that has the specific intent to inflict pain or injury on an opponent. This definition does not include injuries that are a "normal" part of the game. Any injury that results from a normal play within the rules of the game is generally seen as an unfortunate accident—an agreed-upon risk the players knew about when they signed up. When sports commentators and analysts discuss sports violence, they generally do not talk about the type of violence that is accepted as the normal state of play. Instead, they focus on what they consider the "bad" kind of violence—that is, malicious actions taken with the intent to injure an opponent. The distinction, however, between unacceptable and acceptable violence can be hard to make. For example, a hockey player who purposely hits an opposing player in the face with a hockey stick is trying specifically to hurt that person, so this would be considered a violent action that they would receive a penalty for. In contrast, a hockey player who accidentally hits another player in the back of the leg while trying to get the puck away from them is only trying to win the game, so this action is not considered violent according to sports officials; in fact, the player may be praised for their aggressiveness and willingness to "get in there" and do what it takes to stop the other team from winning. Sometimes the distinction between a legal and illegal play is even smaller: A football player can completely level an opposing player in midair, but if they lower their helmet at all, it is an illegal play and carries penalties and even monetary fines, depending on how severe their action was.

The media has played its own role in sports violence by making such violence more visible during the last half of the 20th century. The violence that had always been part of many sports is now seen on television by millions of viewers, and violent actions in sports are frequently praised by analysts.

Common Injuries
head - 14%
face - 7%
finger - 12%
knee - 9%
ankle - 15%

1.35 Million
number of children seen in emergency departments with sports-related injuries in 2012

every **3** minutes, a child is seen in emergency departments for a sports-related concussion

Common Diagnoses
most common diagnoses seen in emergency departments for sports-related injuries

strains and sprains - 451,480
fractures - 249,500
contusions and abrasions - 210,640
concussions - 163,670

Injuries by Sport
for athletes ages 12 to 17 years, 2011

sport	number of players	number of injuries	% of injuries that are concussions
basketball	6,268,000	249,650	7%
soccer	3,780,000	104,190	13%
football	3,246,000	275,050	13%
volleyball	3,246,000	31,460	6%
baseball	2,620,000	61,510	11%
softball	2,163,000	39,070	11%
cheerleading	1,176,000	28,890	12%
wrestling	657,000	33,790	14%
ice hockey	480,000	9,540	31%

Playing sports frequently results in injury, as this information from the nonprofit organization Safe Kids shows.

It is not only professional sports that are seeing an increase in violence. Youth teams are taking their cues from the professionals. More than 30 million children are involved in some form of youth sports in the United States. However, the issue of violence in youth sports has not been studied extensively, and reputable statistics are difficult to find, especially since there are thousands more youth teams than professional ones. This makes studying overall trends very difficult.

Historical Perspective

Sports violence is certainly not a new phenomenon. In many ancient societies, the government's primary goal was to conquer neighboring countries as a way to expand its territory and power. To achieve this goal, the country used a large army of warriors. Violence in these cultures was common and often carried over into sports. Writer Jonathon Hardcastle gave one example: "During the Roman Empire, violence in sports became the generally accepted principle and spectators not only endorsed it, but also embraced it as a social norm."[7]

Historians can trace some sports violence back to the ancient gladiators of Rome, although it is likely that other, older societies played violent sports that are less well documented. A gladiator was a person who was trained to entertain the public by fighting another person or a wild animal to the death in an ancient Roman arena. Generally, a gladiator was a professional combatant, a captive, or a slave; regular citizens were only spectators. If a gladiator was unwilling to be violent in the arena, they would be killed. In order to survive, a gladiator needed to be ruthless.

The first gladiator matches took place in Rome in 264 BC. The sport remained popular, despite the brutalities, for more than 600 years before being abolished. Romans cheered wildly, like modern-day baseball fans, as men fought each other, as well as wild animals, resulting in many brutal, violent deaths.

In addition to gladiator matches, the ancient Greeks and Romans also competed in chariot races, in which drivers raced two-wheeled carts that were pulled by horses. These races had similarities to modern-day NASCAR races. Each race generally featured 40 chariots that ran the length of a track and then

Gladiator Battles in Pop Culture

Many movies and books have centered around gladiators, but some have updated the concept. For example, the book and movie series *The Hunger Games* echoes the ancient gladiator tradition. In this series, which takes place in the United States in a dystopian future, two children from each of the 12 districts into which the country has been split are chosen at random and sent to fight each other on television for entertainment. This series looks at the psychological trauma this kind of contest inflicts on its participants, who must choose to commit unthinkable acts of violence and betrayal if they want to stay alive. Like ancient Roman victors, the winners are viewed as celebrities and given special treatment.

Another updated take on the gladiator concept was included in the movie *Thor: Ragnarok*. When Thor is taken captive by a character called the Grandmaster, he is forced to compete in a gladiatorial battle with the Hulk, who has become the Grandmaster's champion fighter. As in *The Hunger Games*, Thor ends up fighting someone he had previously considered a friend, and the Hulk—who has won every battle up until he fights Thor—is viewed as a hero by the society he lives in. He is celebrated by the general public, and the Grandmaster provides him with the best food and living quarters.

This sign advertising Thor: Ragnarok *includes the Hulk in armor that resembles what gladiators wore in ancient Rome.*

circled back to the starting point. During the course of nearly every event, there were numerous bloody and often fatal accidents as horses and chariots crashed into each other.

Several other ancient sports were also built on violence. An example of such a sport is boxing, which remains popular today but dates back to ancient civilizations in Egypt and the Middle East. In addition, the early Aztecs and Maya of Central America played a variety of ritual games resulting in death for one of the teams. These games were often played as a way to offer a sacrifice to the gods. Tournaments in medieval Europe that involved jousting and sword fighting were designed as training for war and also frequently had fatal consequences.

"Just Part of the Game"

Violence remains part of the modern world of athletics. Some kinds of violence are allowed—or even considered necessary— for particular sports. These violent acts are said to be sanctioned, acceptable, or "legal." Boxing, for instance, has violence at its core; the sole intent in boxing is for a participant to hit their opponent and knock them out before their opponent can do the same to them. Football also has built-in violence that involves tackling, an act of violence done with the intention of stopping a player.

Mixed martial arts (MMA) is another sport in which violence is both sanctioned and expected. It includes elements of boxing, wrestling, and various forms of martial arts. The sport is massively popular today, despite its many critics who claim the sport is too brutal and bloody. A decade ago, such fighting was barely legal, loosely organized street fighting; today, it is a fully regulated sport and one of the fastest-growing and most popular televised sports in the world.

On-the-field fighting is not generally an approved action in most sports. In professional ice hockey, however, fighting is viewed as part of the sport. The unwritten rule in hockey is that every player must come to the aid of a teammate who is bullied, hit, or suffering an injury because of a hard hit, especially if the impacted player is the goalie. This means that when a fight breaks out between two players, it can quickly grow to involve

Mixed martial arts is a brutal but increasingly popular sport.

everyone on the ice. Hockey officials are reluctant to ban fighting because, much like ancient Romans watching gladiator battles, many fans as well as players expect and enjoy it. Officials also believe this kind of "player policing" helps stop other violent acts, such as dangerous hits.

VIOLENCE DOES NOT MAKE HOCKEY BETTER

"Anything that takes one's eye away from the skill and artistry of the best players in the world, in my mind, undermines the product."

–Michael Wilbon, sports journalist, on whether fighting should be eliminated from ice hockey

One of the reasons such acts of violence are allowed in these sports is that the participants have agreed beforehand that these acts are an acceptable part of that particular sport. Written rules have been put into place to prevent other forms of violence from occurring. Referees and umpires are then hired to ensure that the athletes do not break the rules. Football players thus agree that tackling is an approved act, while cheap shots—the name given to violent actions that aim to deliberately hurt an opponent—are not. Penalties are then imposed for those players who take cheap shots.

Hired for Violence

Ice hockey has a long history of violence, both sanctioned and unsanctioned. For years, many teams employed several players who were referred to as the "enforcers" or "goons." These players rarely scored but could be counted on to start fights in the hopes of changing a game's momentum. It was an enforcer's job to bully opposing players and use violence to prevent the other team from playing well. Enforcers frequently left their opponents unconscious on the ice.

The National Hockey League (NHL) began to cut back on this kind of behavior in the 1980s. Concerned about not having a national television contract because of the violence, the league was hoping to improve its image. Officials began severely penalizing players who started fights. By the late 1990s, hockey had somewhat cleaned up its act, with most teams dropping their number of enforcers down to one. The number of fights decreased dramatically. Many of the toughest players, however, continue to be fan favorites. Coaches, in contrast, are less tolerant of such actions, especially during playoff games.

While aggressive play is expected and rewarded, the majority of players try to draw a line between acceptable and unacceptable aggression. In baseball, sliding hard into second base to break up a double play, for instance, is acceptable, while leaving the base path to intentionally knock down a fielder is not. Rushing a quarterback and tackling him before he throws the ball is an acceptable form of violence in football; hitting the quarterback after he has released the ball is not acceptable.

Despite the many safeguards that have been built into the world of sports, even sanctioned violence has its risks, as violence—even actions that are considered normal and acceptable—take an enormous toll on a player's body. In fact, 90 percent of all player injuries occur as a result of sanctioned types of violent contact. Despite the potential for injury, though, many athletes find sanctioned violence and aggression both satisfying and enjoyable.

Against the Rules

Unsanctioned violence is any violent act outside the written and unwritten rules of a particular sport, although some people disagree on which actions can be considered unsanctioned. Part of the reason for so many acts of unsanctioned violence is that most athletes tend to think of the opposing team as the enemy due to the "win at all costs" mentality drilled into players' heads from a young age. By thinking of the opposing team as enemy combatants, a sporting event starts to feel like a war, and the use of violence to interfere with an opposing player's performance becomes acceptable behavior in some players' minds. In any other area of life, these same athletes would likely consider such acts to be immoral, but in sports, they believe anything goes as long as it helps win the game.

Intimidation—trying to scare opponents—and cheap shots have become an ingrained part of many professional sports. A player hitting an opponent with a closed fist, driving a helmet into someone's head or body, and slamming a hockey stick across a rival's back are all examples of unsanctioned violence. Some players have come to equate excellence in their sport with such violence; these players often use unsanctioned acts of violence to prove to coaches and management how tough they are.

Unsanctioned violence also includes deliberately injuring an opponent in an effort to remove that player from the game. Many players, in fact, have gained a reputation due to such acts of violence. Alex Karras, a former Detroit Lions defensive football player, was one such player. Karras once stated, "I had a license to kill for sixty minutes a week. My opponents were all fair game and when I got off the field, I had no regrets."[8]

Both sanctioned and unsanctioned violence tragically result in frequent injuries. The statistics are eye-opening. The Centers for Disease Control and Prevention (CDC) is one organization that keeps statistics on sports injuries. Between 2016 and 2017, it reported, injuries related to high school athletics occurred 1,160,321 times. In addition, the National Collegiate Athletic Association (NCAA) believes that football, in many cases, produces more severe injuries than most other sports. According to the Pro Athlete Law Group, there are 20,718 football injuries within the NCAA each year, 841 of which are spinal injuries. Unfortunately, sometimes student athletes are not even aware of how badly they have been injured, leading them to keep playing and sustaining even worse injuries. For example, the Kansas City Chiefs recruited University of South Carolina student-athlete Stanley Doughty upon graduation, but the mandatory health exam for new players ended his career before it started when an X-ray revealed that Doughty had a cervical spine injury. The Pro Athlete Law Group explained, "Sadly, Doughty did not know the severity of his injuries because the doctors at his school had cleared him to continue playing. During his college football career, an impact left him temporarily paralyzed with a tingling sensation in his arms and neck, but the neurosurgeon gave Doughty the 'go-ahead' to keep playing."[9] This decision placed him in great danger, but luckily, he escaped further paralysis.

With injuries so common, the average playing career for professional football players lasts about two and a half years—down from about five years in 2008—making a football career the shortest of all professional sports careers. This trend suggests that players are less willing than they were in the past to ignore the damage to their bodies and brains, regardless of pressure from team officials.

Types of Unsanctioned Violence

Although nearly all sports include some form of violence, both sanctioned and unsanctioned, the form that violence takes

Concussion Diagnosis by School Year, 2005/06–2016/17

	2005-06	2006-07	2007-08	2008-09	2009-10	2010-11
total number of injuries	1,44,172	1,466,389	1,414,139	1,248,126	1,359,897	1,191,484
percent of injuries that were concussions	9.1%	8.4%	9.2%	11.8%	14.0%	20.0%

	2011-12	2012-13	2013-14	2014-15	2015-16	2016-17
total number of injuries	1,392,262	1,360,701	1,427,315	1,194,932	1,391,729	1,157,001
percent of injuries that were concussions	22.2%	23.1%	21.9%	24.6%	24.6%	24.8%

Despite efforts to keep high school athletes safe, the number of concussion injuries has been increasing for more than a decade. This information from the 2016/17 National High School Sports-Related Injury Surveillance Study *outlines the percentage of injuries reported by high school athletes each school year that are concussions.*

differs from sport to sport. In football, for instance, cheap shots are not uncommon. These actions include things such as hitting another player with fists, kicking a player while they are on the ground, using one's helmet to hit another player, gouging another player's eyes, and utilizing blindside hits, in which a player deliberately hits or tackles an opponent who is up in the air catching a ball or has his back turned while passing. Some football players believe that such violence is just part of the game, but others consider it to be unfair and unnecessary.

Cheap shots frequently end with injuries—sometimes severe—for the unsuspecting victim. For example, during a preseason game in 1978, Darryl Stingley, a wide receiver for the New England Patriots, went high in the air to catch a pass; he missed the ball. Jack Tatum, nicknamed "The Assassin," slammed into Stingley while he was midair and belted him in the head with a padded forearm. The blow broke Stingley's neck and paralyzed the 26-year-old from the neck down. Football officials did not call a penalty, nor did Tatum ever offer a formal apology, although he admitted once that his best hits bordered on assault—a crime that would carry jail time if he performed those hits off the field.

Even sanctioned violence in football can lead to catastrophic injuries. In 2007, special teams player Kevin Everett of the Buffalo Bills attempted to tackle a player during a routine kickoff return. The normally relatively harmless play resulted in a devastating neck injury for Everett that almost caused him to become permanently paralyzed. While he eventually regained the ability to walk, his football career was over from the moment the hit took place.

Kevin Everett escaped permanent paralysis when he was tackled in 2007, but his football career ended for good.

Sometimes careers are ended through simple but violent accidents. In 2011, for instance, Chicago Bears player Johnny Knox was trying to recover a fumble when he accidentally hit Seattle Seahawks player Anthony Hargrove head-on. Knox required emergency surgery to stabilize his spine, and although he, too, avoided permanent paralysis, he remains unable to walk without a limp or stand for long periods of time.

Those who play college football also commit acts of unsanctioned violence. A total of 12 Clemson University and University of South Carolina football players, for example, were suspended one game after a brawl broke out in November 2004. Clemson senior player Yusef Kelly was seen kicking a South Carolina player who was lying facedown with his helmet off. Both sidelines cleared as all the players rushed to the field. The NCAA acted quickly in suspending many of the players, stating that the athletes had violated the rules of good sportsmanship.

RISK MAKES THE SPORT BETTER

"There is risk involved in boxing, as in all sports in which physical contact is involved ... To remove all the risk would be turning boxing into something quite different than the sport as we know it—and I do not think anyone would want that, least of all the boxers themselves."

–Graham Houston, journalist and editor of *Boxing Monthly*

Graham Houston, "Graham the Ring Has Long Been a Part of Boxing," ESPN, November 14, 2007. sports.espn.go.com/sports/boxing/news/story?id=3107450.

Other sports also have their own share of unsanctioned violence. Pushing, grappling, and punching matches take place all the time at all levels of hockey, and while fights are technically not allowed, they are expected and often enjoyed by fans. More serious, however, are unsanctioned incidents in which faces are split open by hockey skate blades, heads are smashed by a hockey stick, or blind hits are made that lead to severe injury. Even though players today are protected by helmets and other equipment, they continue to have their jaws broken and their teeth knocked out; they also suffer concussions and paralysis. Even young players are sometimes encouraged to fight if another player provokes them. Because fights are seen as part of the game of hockey, there are certain "rules of engagement" that participants in the fight are expected to follow. If a fight breaks out during a hockey game, etiquette requires that players throw down their sticks and fight only with their fists.

Basketball is another sport with the potential for unsanctioned forms of violence. In the early days of basketball, however, its inventor, James A. Naismith, did not envision the sport

While technically not allowed, fights in hockey are part of the reason why fans enjoy the sport.

as being violent; in fact, he wanted above all else to avoid physical contact. Knowing that players might get rough, however, Naismith put in place penalties for tripping and other contact fouls, all forms of accidental violence. As basketball grew in popularity and became a professional sport, however, salaries climbed into the millions and winning became more important so teams could keep financially rewarding sponsorships. With so much at stake, the game became more physical and more violent, with more unsanctioned violence such as pushing, shoving, and obvious fouls, including hitting a player while they are in the air or punching a player at any time. Players continue to get bigger, stronger, and faster, and the potential for serious injury and damage during fights rises.

On November 19, 2004, arguably the most infamous fight in National Basketball Association (NBA) history occurred. The incident, a bench-clearing brawl between the

Detroit Pistons and Indiana Pacers, has since been dubbed the "Malice at the Palace." Pistons center Ben Wallace was fouled by Pacers forward Ron Artest on a shot attempt. Artest saw the foul as unnecessary and malicious, so he became angry at Wallace, who defended his actions. As the two players yelled at each other and shoved one another, a fan threw a drink from the stands, hitting Artest. Artest then climbed into the stands, going after the offending fan, which started a huge fight between players and fans that lasted for several minutes. The event led to multiple legal charges for players and fans alike, as well as sanctions from the NBA itself, with a total of nine players receiving suspensions for a total of 146 games, losing a total of nearly $11 million in salary. "It's the ugliest thing I've seen as a coach or player," Pistons coach Larry Brown later said. "I'm just embarrassed for our league and disappointed for our young people to see that."[10]

Unsanctioned violence happens occasionally in baseball as well. The most common unsanctioned violent act in baseball is when the pitcher throws a beanball, which is the term for a ball that is intentionally aimed at the hitter's head. While it is considered acceptable to brush back, or throw a pitch close to the batter to "brush" them away from their normal stance, actually hitting the batter is not allowed. Severe injuries such as concussions and even deaths have occurred as a result of beanballs. Another form of unsanctioned violence involves running into opponents and deliberately using the spikes on one's shoes to hurt them. In some cases, baseball players also get into bench-clearing brawls on the field.

While most of the violence seen in boxing is sanctioned and considered part of the sport, there have been numerous incidents in which the violence has shifted into unsanctioned territory. One of the most well-known incidents involved former heavyweight champion Mike Tyson. Tyson, while praised for his ferocious boxing style, was also infamous for his controversial behavior outside the ring. In 1992, for instance, he was tried and convicted of sexual assault and rape, serving three years in prison for his crime. Following his release, Tyson attempted a comeback. Part of that comeback involved a fight for the

A Significant Moment of Violence

One of the most notorious incidents of unsanctioned violence in professional basketball occurred on December 9, 1977. The media has since referred to the incident as "The Punch." Sports author John Feinstein described it as "a watershed moment in sports, because it has become *the* symbol of what can happen when fights break out among very strong, very athletic young men."[1]

In a game between the Los Angeles Lakers and the Houston Rockets, a large fight broke out on the floor involving the Lakers' star center, Kareem Abdul-Jabbar, and one of the Rockets' players. Kermit Washington, one of Abdul-Jabbar's teammates, came to his assistance. Out of the corner of his eye, Washington saw Rockets player Rudy Tomjanovich running at full speed toward the fight. Reacting instantaneously, Washington threw a punch at Tomjanovich, catching him on the jaw and face. Tomjanovich appeared to fly backward before landing unconscious on the floor, blood streaming out of his nose. The punch had landed with such devastating force that everyone in the arena had heard the sound of bones breaking.

Paul Toffel, the doctor who later saw Tomjanovich in the hospital, compared the injuries to "those suffered by someone thrown through the windshield of a car traveling 50 miles per hour."[2] X-rays showed extensive injuries to the face, nose, and jaw. The top part of Tomjanovich's skull was actually out of alignment, which could easily have killed him. He later had a total of five surgeries to repair the damage.

Both men returned to basketball but were never the same. Their play suffered, as did Washington's reputation. As a result of the incident, the NBA increased fines for fighting and also began issuing longer suspensions for such behavior. The league added a third official to referee each game in hopes of stopping violent behavior before it reached the stage of actual punches being thrown.

1. John Feinstein, *The Punch*. New York, NY: Back Bay, 2002, p. xiv.
2. Feinstein, *The Punch*, p. 6.

heavyweight title with Evander Holyfield. During the fight, Tyson was disqualified for biting off part of Holyfield's ear and spitting it on the mat. As a result of this incident, his boxing license was taken away, and he eventually retired from boxing.

The Role of the Media

Many sports experts partially blame the media for the rise of unsanctioned violence in sports. "If it bleeds, it leads," is an old saying among journalists. This means that people are drawn to shocking stories, especially violent ones, so news outlets often cover these stories first to keep viewers interested in the show. While some people have criticized what they see as the sensationalism of violence, others argue that television is simply giving the public what it wants. They believe that if people did not want to see such violence, they would not watch it, and then news outlets would lead with a different type of story.

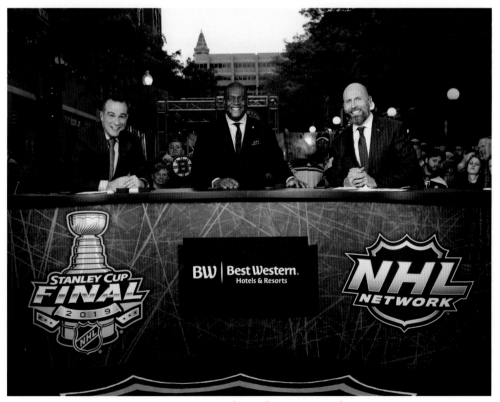

Many sports commentators argue that violence in sports draws more viewers.

Some people agree that violence is a key part of why fans watch sports. According to Fred Engh, founder of the National Alliance for Youth Sports, "Especially in this era driven by ratings, the story has become not about who hit a ninth-inning homer last night, but who purposely hit another player with a pitch to ignite a bench-clearing brawl."[11] In some cases, this appears to be true. For example, in 2012, *The Atlantic* reported that as hockey becomes more violent, more people watch. However, the same article noted that this may be due less to the fights and more to the fact that NHL games are available on more channels than they have been in the past. In other cases, more rigorous studies have shown that violence is not as much of a draw anymore. For example, many NASCAR fans have a reputation for watching mainly to see the eye-catching explosions that happen when a car crashes—as they frequently do. In fact, until recently, each crash boosted viewership by 6 percent. However, according to a study by the University of Iowa, the number of people who watch the sport for the crashes has declined since 2004, when NASCAR introduced a system called the Chase for the Cup, "in which the top ten drivers had their points re-set with ten races to go and only those ten were eligible for the championship."[12] Before this system was put in place, fans could tell early on in the season who would win the championship, so they grew bored with the races and watched mainly for the excitement of the crashes. Increasing the drama and suspense of the sport decreased fans' interest in violence.

THE RISK IS NOT WORTH THE EXCITEMENT

"When the surest way to win (a sporting event) is by damaging the opponent's brain, and this becomes the standard procedure, the sport is morally wrong."

–George D. Lundberg, a member of the American Medical Association

Analysts who disagree with the notion that the media negatively influences violence in sports argue that violent behavior is present in everyday life and that it is just another part of sports. They further declare that violence has not increased since sports became televised, but that instead, people are more aware of it because they can see it happening in front of them instead of hearing about it later—or never hearing about it at all. These analysts insist that violence has been around longer than television has. While some studies show that watching violence makes people more violent to those around them, others show that it does not. This is an ongoing field of study, and there are no answers that can be applied to every situation.

In fact, some sports analysts believe that watching violence on the field or court actually provides an alternative to other types of violence in society. People who hold this view say that sports violence provides a healthy way for viewers to deal with frustrations and aggressions. While some studies have been done on this matter, their methods have been flawed. For instance, a survey taken in 1987—a time when professional football was not being televised because of a players' strike—showed that some families experienced more domestic violence. Some analysts concluded that this increase in domestic violence was directly related to the absence of football. However, when interpreting studies, it is important to remember that correlation does not equal causation. In other words, just because two things are happening at the same time—for example, the increase in the number of hockey fights and the increase in hockey viewership—that does not mean one is causing the other. No recent studies have been done into the connection between sports and domestic violence, but domestic violence experts say that abusers are rarely influenced by outside forces; things such as the absence of a sporting game or the presence of alcohol do not cause abuse, although they have the potential to make it worse. For instance, a 2009 study by the National Bureau of Economic Research found that when a football game ends in an upset, the losing team's home state briefly experiences more domestic violence than usual. This indicates not that football creates abusers, but that a football fan who is already abusive may take out their frustration about the results of a game on those closest to them.

Another study, this one published in 2018 in the *Journal of Sports Economics*, reported that property and drug crime decreases as much as 25 percent during televised sporting events. However, rather than suggesting the violence of the sport decreases crime, the results imply that criminals would rather watch their favorite sport than commit crimes. The connection between sports violence and violence that occurs in everyday life is unclear, but so far no studies have proven that sports violence has positive effects, despite some claims to the contrary.

Violence in Youth Sports

One of the most common complaints by people who claim that the media focuses too much on sports violence is that such violence is damaging to today's youth. Millions of children and young adults watch sports on television. Psychological research has shown that young children model their behavior and attitudes on those of adults, particularly people they admire, such as sports stars. When children see their favorite sports stars committing violent acts, they can easily become confused. Most know that such violent acts are disapproved of by society under normal circumstances, but they also see such acts being praised and repeatedly replayed on television. Teens, some people fear, may then imitate violent athletes when they play informal games and organized youth sports.

Although no studies have confirmed that simply watching sports makes people behave more violently than they would otherwise, several studies have backed up the idea that young athletes are more likely to behave violently off the field as well as on it. A 1996 study by the University of North Carolina reported that an increasing number of young athletes identified violence as a normal part of sports. The study did not make a distinction between sanctioned or unsanctioned violence. In 2008, Penn State University assistant professor of sociology Derek Kreager "used a national database of about 7000 students from 120 schools to examine a variety of issues, including popularity, self-esteem and propensity for violence."[13] To measure propensity for violence, Kreager looked at how many students had been disciplined for fighting at school. By looking at participants in multiple different sports, he was able to identify that "football players and wrestlers have a 40 percent greater chance of being involved in a serious fight than all other athletes,"[14] especially those whose friends were mainly other football players or wrestlers. However, a key question that the study could not answer is, do sports that involve violence cause players to be more violent, or do they attract people who have a propensity for violence in the first place? More research is needed to come to a concrete conclusion, but Kreager came to a preliminary conclusion: Kids who had been violent before joining a team were more likely to be wrestlers, while kids who joined the football team were more likely to become violent after joining the team, suggesting that the sport itself makes the issue worse.

Research has shown that football players are among the most likely athletes to engage in violence off the field.

Some sociologists and psychologists believe that adding to the problem of violence in youth sports is the fact that a number of parents are putting too much pressure on their children to win, or at least to perform well. Some children have schedules for sports that include practices early in the morning and late at night, practice every day after school, and games several times a week. This allows little time for homework or time with the family. This pressure from parents can sometimes cause children to play more aggressively and act in a violent way in order to impress their parents and succeed in their sport. When they are at the games themselves, these parents often yell instructions at their children from the stands, reinforcing the idea that they need to win no matter what.

While some see an increase in violence in sports, others argue that it has always been present and is no cause for alarm. Experts are increasingly examining the relationship between aggression and competition, looking for a reason why unsanctioned violence occurs in sports and why some athletes are more prone to violence in their everyday lives.

CHAPTER 2

Violence and Competition

Winning is frequently seen as the most important aspect of any athletic competition, and this is drilled into athletes' heads from a very young age. In the minds of some players, anything is justified if it allows their team to win. Athletes are told to play through injuries because "pain is weakness leaving the body"—an attitude that has led to lifelong consequences for some. Athletes believe they need to do whatever is necessary to secure the win so they do not let down their teammates, their coaches, or their fans. The increased use of violence, both sanctioned and unsanctioned, in contact sports is a natural progression of this frame of mind. Athletes are taught to accept no limits in attaining success. This pressure to succeed can come from many sources: coaches, fans, management, and athletes themselves, as well.

Some sociologists and psychologists believe that young athletes learn about aggression and violence early in their athletic careers and are conditioned, or trained through repeated actions and messages, to develop aggressive behaviors. Author John H. Kerr theorized that when young players first become involved in a team contact sport, they find that they enjoy the activity; as they continue to play, the level of physicality and aggression generally increases alongside the increased skill of the players. As more time passes, the physical domination of opposing athletes becomes crucial both to team success and the athlete's enjoyment of the sport. The players learn that violent and aggressive acts are often rewarded by praise from coaches, fans, and other players. Eventually, according to Kerr, an "excessive appetite for ... violence in a team sport becomes the major source of pleasure in an athlete's life."[15]

Many athletes are taught from a young age that the only thing that matters in athletic competition is winning, even if it is never spoken out loud.

It has long been thought that participation in a sport allows children and young adults an outlet for their aggression: If they are being active and violent out on the field, the thinking goes, they will not feel the need to be violent and aggressive outside the context of the sport. In recent years, though, this concept has begun to undergo a reevaluation. Studies have proven that any physical activity provides a benefit by releasing endorphins, which are chemicals the body produces to naturally reduce feelings of pain and stress. This is why regular exercise is often part of the treatment plan for mental illnesses such as depression and anxiety. Because of this, some people believe that in addition to releasing endorphins, competition between sports teams has the added benefit of providing an outlet through which people can release aggressive tendencies. Other sports experts challenge this, believing instead that rather than reducing normal aggression, participating in aggressive sports often makes players act even more aggressively in other circumstances.

Is Winning the Only Important Thing?

The need to win was most clearly expressed by legendary Green Bay Packers football coach Vince Lombardi when he said, "Winning isn't everything. It's the only thing."[16] As a result, inhibitions are sometimes put aside in an effort to win at any cost. If violence is needed to earn a win, then so be it. Coaches and other players may even reject and ridicule team members who fail to use violence to gain an edge. Players who do not play aggressively and dominate the other team are often called "soft" as an insult.

National Football League (NFL) coach Vince Lombardi (center), the namesake of the NFL championship trophy, was famously obsessed with winning at all costs—a mentality he passed on to the men he coached.

Individual athletes sometimes take winning so seriously that competitors are intentionally injured. In one high-profile incident, for example, figure skater and Olympic favorite Nancy Kerrigan was assaulted after a practice session in a Detroit arena. Kerrigan was hit across the right leg and knee by a man who later claimed he was hired by rival skater Tonya Harding's then-husband and her bodyguard. Harding later admitted to wanting Kerrigan out of the Olympics so that she could win, but she never admitted direct involvement in planning the assault. Despite the injury, Kerrigan went on to win the silver medal at the Olympic Games. Harding was sentenced to three years' probation and was banned forever from participating in skating events run by the U.S. Figure Skating Association. This incident was examined in a 2017 movie called *I, Tonya*, which was based on interviews with Harding and her former husband.

The need to win in sports that Harding felt begins very early. Players in youth leagues often receive the same message: Be number one; win at all costs. Sometimes children are not told this directly but rather learn it by observing the adults around them. For example, a coach who tells their team that winning is not as important as having fun is sending a very different message if they get angry at the team when they lose or if they only put the best players in the game and let the less talented ones sit on the sidelines.

Sometimes coaches send the message that violence is acceptable if it allows the team to win. For instance, Engh once met with some nine-year-old football players prior to a game. One told him, "Coach told us that if we can put the [opposing team's] quarterback out of the game, they won't stand a chance against us."[17] Engh commented, "At the age of nine, these children were being indoctrinated into the philosophy that winning at all costs

SENDING THE WRONG MESSAGE

"A major justification for our ... enormous investment in competitive sports is that 'sports build character, teach team effort, and encourage sportsmanship and fair play' ... Instead of learning fair play and teamwork, too many of our children are learning winning is everything."

–Canadian Centres for Teaching Peace

Performance-Enhancing Drugs

The "win at all costs" mindset can damage more than just a person's self-esteem. In some cases, it can have negative effects on health as well. When the pressure to continue winning becomes too great, some players turn to performance-enhancing drugs to help them stay on top. Taking performance-enhancing drugs is known as "doping."

Athletes who use drugs do so because they believe the drugs are necessary to help them remain competitive. Many youth athletes are also influenced when they see professionals—especially baseball players—using performance-enhancing drugs such as steroids and achieving great athletic feats. However, while steroids can help build bulky muscles, they do not guarantee improved athletic ability and can lead to long-term heart, liver, and reproductive problems.

Each professional sports league, as well as amateur sports organizations, now has its own set of rules regarding drug testing, along with different levels of punishment for first, second, and third offenses. While mandatory drug testing has been required in a number of professional and amateur sports, testing cannot always detect all illegal substances. One of the most famous doping scandals of all time involved legendary cyclist and multiple time Tour de France winner Lance Armstrong. His use of performance-enhancing drugs went undetected for years, even after countless tests. His doping was finally brought to public light in 2012, after a former fellow competitor named him as part of a lawsuit.

was the only thing that mattered, and that cheating and brutality were not only acceptable forms of behavior, but virtuous acts when they lead to the all-important goal of winning."[18] In fact, according to a survey done by the Minnesota Amateur Sports Commission, more than 8 percent of players admitted they had been told or pressured to intentionally hurt another player in order to win a game.

As children age, sports competition generally gets more serious. Kids who play just for the fun of it often drop out because of the increased pressure to win each game.

Critics argue that children who cannot live up to the pressure of always winning may lose self-esteem. Many children, in fact, quit youth sports because of such pressure. The Canadian Centres for Teaching Peace reported, "The emphasis on winning deprives youth of the pleasure of playing the game."[19]

Some youth coaches, however, do not believe winning is everything. There are numerous examples of coaches who teach good sportsmanship and character; they send the message that children should have fun on the athletic field because ultimately, they are playing a game, not going to war.

While coaches certainly can contribute to the winning-at-all-costs attitude, other factors also impact young players. Some young athletes feel pressure from teammates to win and rely on violent actions to accomplish that goal. Nobody wants to feel like they were the one who let down the team, so when teammates start accusing each other instead of supporting each other after a loss, it can contribute to violent actions in future games. A number of young players, in their desire to win scholarships and earn a spot on college or professional teams, may also resort to violence in order to impress coaches. For many young athletes who come from low-income families, their sport is their way out of a dangerous neighborhood; for some, it may be the only way they can afford to go to college, so the stakes are higher. However, low-income players are not the only ones who resort to violence on the playing field.

Many coaches teach good sportsmanship. This attitude must be reinforced early and often for young athletes.

The pressure to win continues at the collegiate and professional level as well. By that time, many players have been well indoctrinated into the winning-is-everything philosophy. In a study that investigated perceptions of violence in sports, researchers Larry M. Lance and Charlynn E. Ross discovered that "stress on winning at any cost has brought about increased acceptance of violence as a means to achieve that end."[20]

Athletes as Warriors

The focus on winning, some experts believe, has also resulted in players who are not just athletes but "warriors" as well. Lynn Jamieson and Thomas Orr explained, "The warrior athlete represents the ideals of our culture. Athletes are encouraged to embrace violence and aggression as a tool of the trade. Athletes and spectators are groomed to celebrate big hits, dangerous plays, and fights between players as a necessary part of the game. Hitting opponents and having large scale fights on the field is often accepted."[21]

A number of sports experts link the warrior athlete attitude to an exaggerated sense of masculine pride. They believe that sports aggression is almost exclusively a male behavior and suggest that any defeat in the athletic arena may be seen as a severe blow to the athlete's manhood. From a young age, boys taunt each other in sports by saying things such as, "You hit like a girl," establishing the threat of loss of manhood early on. Jay Coakley explained, "In many societies today, participation in power and performance sports has become an important way to prove masculinity ... Boys and men who play ... sports learn quickly that they are evaluated in terms of their ability to do violence in combination with physical skills."[22] As a result, violence is thought to be one way to protect one's pride and masculinity.

However, others disagree with this view, noting that there are numerous instances of both sanctioned and unsanctioned violence by female athletes. For example, roller derby is one of the few female-dominated sports in the world, and it is inherently violent. The goal in roller derby is for one team member, known as the jammer, to fight her way through the rest of the players—known as blockers—as they form a pack to prevent the other jammer from getting through while at the same time helping their own jammer get ahead. This leads to a lot of pushing, shoving, and other sanctioned violence, but penalties are also given when unsanctioned violence occurs.

In most other women's sports leagues, however, violence tends to be less common because it carries stricter penalties in many women's sports leagues than in men's sports leagues. For example, while body checking is allowed in men's hockey, it is not allowed in women's hockey. When a female athlete does commit unsanctioned violence, it is generally sensationalized in the media. One high-profile instance occurred in 2009, when University of New Mexico soccer player Elizabeth Lambert shoved, punched, and pulled an opponent to the ground by her ponytail. Women's sports are typically given very little media coverage, but this event put women's sports in the national news. According to the *New York Times*, the video of Lambert's violent actions "spurred a national debate about sportsmanship, gender roles, double standards regarding aggressiveness and news media coverage and the sexualized portrayal of female athletes."[23] Lambert was suspended, but public opinion was split; some fans wanted her banned from playing, while others believed she was doing her job as a defender. Many people on both sides also sexualized the incident—something that is generally not seen in discussions of violence between male athletes. According to Pat Griffin, professor of social justice education at the University of Massachusetts, this helps "trivialize, or make less threatening, women's sports."[24]

Many commentators noted that, while male athletes are typically celebrated for violent actions during a game, female athletes tend to be held to a different standard. Anson Dorrance, a women's soccer coach, summed up the double standard by saying, "It's almost like they crossed a gender line they weren't allowed to cross, like we want to take them out of the athletic arena and put them in the nurturing, caring role as mothers of children."[25] Other violent or aggressive actions by female athletes—such as angry speeches given by tennis champion Serena Williams and a 2010 fistfight between Baylor University basketball players—have been similarly sensationalized by the media. The question of whether violence in sports is justified seems to become more complicated when the athletes are women.

ANGER IS NOT JUST A MALE EMOTION

"We have people with anger problems throughout the world and some of these are women; why wouldn't there be some of those represented in the athletic population? Of course there would be ... but what is being done? ... It is our society tolerating violence that is the most predictable reinforcer [of athletes' violent behavior]."

–Dr. Mitch Abrams, sports psychologist

The Role of Fans and Management

The concept of the sports star as a warrior is constantly reinforced with specific word usage, such as battling, blitz, trenches, attack, sacked, etc. Coakley explained, "Professional athletes are entertainers, and they [sports management] now use a promotional and heroic rhetoric that presents images of revenge, retaliation, hate, hostility, intimidation, aggression, violence, domination, and destruction."[26]

The image of the warrior athlete is a profitable one for professional sports leagues. The NFL, NHL, and NBA, for instance, all use these kinds of images to promote their games. Advertisements for big upcoming sporting events, such as ice hockey's Stanley Cup Final and the Super Bowl in professional football, frequently contain footage of violent hits. Marketers argue that such images attract larger audiences—an outcome that generates more profits. Are people drawn to sports because of the violence, because of the excitement of watching skilled athletes perform well, or out of the pride they feel when they see their team win? Sociologists and other experts continue to debate this question.

Profit is the primary goal for the management of professional sports teams. Television contracts run into the millions of dollars, so the difference between a winning season and a losing season can translate into large amounts of money for all involved. Because of this, players are often encouraged to use any tactic, including violence, to help their team win and generate more profit through fan interest and ticket sales. Sellouts and packed stadiums are generally the rule for teams that win consistently. Winning teams also appear more often on television than teams that frequently lose.

A team's fans can also increase the tendency toward violence. For example, ice hockey fans often attend games because of the potential for violence. A'Don Allen, sports director for a news channel in Elmira, New York, noted, "The entire arena erupts with cheering when there are fights. Even if their team is losing, the fans still get excited when they see two players pummeling each other."[27]

Violence in Sports as Enforcement

When a player that has been taught their entire life that winning is everything out on the playing field, exerting themselves against the top athletes in the sport—with fans and coaches screaming at them—can often feel like they are fighting for their lives in the Roman Colosseum. It is no wonder that violence can often get out of hand. With players laser-focused on winning, rage—generally in the form of violent retaliation—is sometimes the result. A player or team, for instance, may decide to retaliate against another player or team when they feel that a violent act against themselves or another member of their team was not appropriately penalized, or punished, by the referees. Retaliation is essentially returning an action—hurting someone who hurt you.

Players from several different sports engage in acts of retaliation and consider them a normal part of the sport. In baseball, for instance, a pitcher sometimes purposely hits a batter with the baseball in order to retaliate for an earlier act of violence committed by an opposing pitcher. Sometimes the pitcher decides on this move; other times it is the manager who calls for a pitch aimed at the batter's head to teach the other player or team a lesson. This practice is common at all levels of baseball, but especially Major League Baseball (MLB). While it is often difficult to determine whether a pitch thrown at a player's head is intentional or not, baseball's record book lists dozens of pitchers who have been labeled as "headhunters" for their history of deliberately throwing at other players. More recently, the head varsity coach of Allegeny-Limestone High School in New York was suspended indefinitely in May 2010 for ordering one of his pitchers to throw at an opposing player.

This kind of retaliation can be dangerous. Pitchers control a very hard ball that can be thrown at speeds of more than 100 miles (161 km) per hour. The potential for serious injury increases dramatically when the ball connects with a batter's head, even if players are wearing helmets. In one tragic incident, Cleveland Indians batter Ray Chapman was hit in the head by a pitch thrown by Carl Mays of the New York Yankees in 1920. Chapman's head was split open, and he died less than 14 hours later.

As of 2019, Ray Chapman (shown here) is the only player in MLB history to die from an in-game injury.

Acts of retaliation also occur frequently in ice hockey—sometimes with tragic consequences. On February 16, 2004, for instance, Steve Moore, a player with the Colorado Avalanche, injured Vancouver Canucks team captain Markus Näslund by knocking him in the head with his elbow. No penalty was called on the play despite the fact that Näslund suffered a concussion and ended up missing three games. While the hit drew criticism from the Canucks players, the NHL ruled that the hit was legal.

Vancouver players, however, would not let the matter rest. Canucks general manager Brad May urged his team to take revenge against Moore; he stated, "There's definitely a bounty on his head … It's going to be fun when we get him."[28] The retaliation came in a game on March 8, 2004. Canucks player Todd Bertuzzi, who had a reputation for violent hits, was sent on the ice late in the third period. After failing to get Moore to fight with him, Bertuzzi skated after him and punched Moore in the head from behind and then fell on him, along with several other players from both teams. Moore's head was driven into the ice, causing three fractured neck vertebrae, facial cuts, and a concussion. He lay on the ice, unconscious, for more than 10 minutes, and he never played hockey again. Bertuzzi was immediately suspended for the remainder of the season and had to reapply for reinstatement the next season.

Most sociologists and sports psychologists agree that more steps must be taken to prevent further incidents. However, even with penalties for retaliation in place, it is difficult to prevent someone from being injured by a player who cares more about getting revenge than being penalized.

In stock car racing, drivers often bump other cars, intending to force the opposing drivers out of the race. This can lead to deadly crashes.

What Is Sportsmanship?

With such an emphasis on winning and with an increased amount of violence in sports, many sports experts have begun to question where sportsmanship fits into the sports equation. Sportsmanship is generally defined as a standard of conduct in which athletes pursue victory in a courteous and fair way, or playing the "right way." Sports can provide an exceptional setting for learning and character development—as long as this expectation is set in the earliest stages of the sport.

Coaches, teammates, parents, siblings, and friends can all contribute to the way a player views their sport. The Josephson Institute, a group dedicated to improving the ethical quality of society, believes that there are six essential elements of character building and sportsmanship that sports can embody: trustworthiness, respect, responsibility, fairness, caring, and citizenship. Trustworthiness involves never cheating and honoring the rules of the sport. An athlete who has respect can win or lose with class, which means showing appreciation for their opponent and honoring the calls made by officials. Responsibility includes maintaining safe conditions on the playing field and being a role model for other players and younger people. Playing by the rules and treating everyone properly are evidence of fairness; ensuring the safety and welfare of other athletes encompasses caring. Finally, being a good citizen includes doing things the right way on the field of play.

SETTING POSITIVE EXPECTATIONS

"While striving to win, children learn about teamwork, leadership and sportsmanship, all of which can contribute to their development as solid citizens. In organized team sports, children work together to accomplish a task and learn from their mistakes. These lessons directly translate into the classroom and beyond."

–Stephen D. Keener, president and chief executive officer of Little League International

Sportsmanship can often go by the wayside when a team's emphasis is all about winning. This can happen at all levels of the game, but it is highly visible in the professional leagues. When young players try to act like their sports heroes and are encouraged in this attitude by the people around them, it can decrease the value they place on sportsmanlike behavior. Kerr further elaborates on sportsmanship in youth sports, saying,

The same kind of attitude from sport education that drives young athletes and teams to focus on defeating opponents also encour-

ages them to think of their participation in sport purely from their own point of view. Opponents are disparaged [mocked] and some coaches even try to foster in their athletes an active dislike for other competitors.[29]

If winning is emphasized above all else, sportsmanship falls by the wayside. There is no place for respectful play if the only goal is to win the game or competition. It is important for players to remember and to reinforce to each other that they are ultimately playing a game, not fighting a war. If this mindset can be established early, perhaps some of the violence in sports today can be decreased in the future.

Violence Off the Field

Although violence within a sports game can be concerning, violence outside the game is even more troubling to experts. Some people excuse violence as long as it serves to help their team win, saying that it is all part of the game and that players knew what they were getting into when they signed up. However, the same behaviors off the field—committed against people who have not agreed to any such thing—is not considered acceptable, even by the people who think violence has a place in sports.

Football players are some of the most likely to become violent off the field. In fact, in a survey done by researchers Jeff Benedict and Don Yaeger, it was found that one in five NFL players surveyed during the 1996–1997 season had been charged with some kind of serious criminal act. In 1997 alone, 38 players in the NFL were arrested for violent crimes. However, other athletes have committed violent crimes as well. The analysts also collected data on NBA players during the 2001–2002 season and discovered that 40 percent of them had a police record involving a serious crime.

These acts are not exclusive to professional athletes. Researchers have also discovered that college athletes are more likely than other students to be accused of rape, assault, break-ins, and drug trafficking. According to Derek Kreager's research, which focused only on male students to eliminate confusion over the gendered double standard, this is due in large part to the culture surrounding a sport. He explained, "The culture of a tennis player is different than the culture of a football player. The tennis player is less likely to get into a fight. I suggest the reason is they don't have an identity that revolves around physical violence."[30] Kreager also found that when students who are not on the football team make friends and spend time with football players, the non-players are more likely to commit violent acts in an effort to impress the players. This finding backs up a 2006 study by Kathleen Miller of the University at Buffalo. She found "a strong correlation between violence and 'jock identity'—that is, a young person, whether on a team or not, who identifies himself as a jock."[31]

Sportswriter John Feinstein summarized the problem of off-the-field violence committed by athletes who play a sport with a high amount of sanctioned violence. He said, "There is no question that there is a problem in a sport where you are told all week to work yourself into a fever pitch to go out and commit violence and then told, once you're off the field, that that's not part of your life. Most athletes can separate the two, but some of them clearly can't."[32]

Violence Against Women

Violent crimes against women account for a troubling portion of off-the-field incidents. The rates of domestic violence are high among professional football players in particular. In 2014, *Sports Illustrated* reported that between 2012 and 2014 alone, 33 NFL players had been arrested for crimes such as domestic violence, assault, and murder; half of these crimes were committed against women.

The issue of domestic violence committed by NFL players came into the public eye in 2014, when Baltimore Ravens running back Ray Rice was caught on video knocking his then-fiancée unconscious in an elevator. Since then, the media has been quicker to highlight stories of other players who have been charged with domestic violence, but the problem has persisted. Some people believe this is due to lenient treatment by the league and fans alike. In 2018, an article by Dayana Sarkisova on the sports website SBNation described the cycle that takes place whenever such an accusation becomes public: "Men hit women,

NFL teams look the other way, we cry out, and the game plays on, until the next woman suffers a blow … Then we begin the process anew."[33] The NFL's policy as of early 2019 is to suspend first-time offenders for six games without pay. After a second offense, the NFL's policy is to permanently ban players. However, these policies are not enforced as often as many might assume, or loopholes in the rules are found. Many teams are willing to pick up good players who will help the team win and ignore what goes on in their personal lives. In one recent example, linebacker Reuben Foster was let go by the San Francisco 49ers after his second domestic violence charge. Several days later, he was signed to Washington's NFL team.

Ray Rice was fired from the Baltimore Ravens after videos of his abusive actions surfaced. Four years later, he said in an interview that he hated the person he had been when he was playing football and partially blamed his abusiveness on the pressures of being a star.

The willingness of the NFL to show leniency to players, many say, encourages them to keep committing crimes. Without any real penalties, they have no incentive to change their behavior. Although Washington released a statement explaining that Foster would have to face a legal investigation and counseling for his behavior, many fans believe this is not good enough. As

Sarkisova wrote, "There is absolutely no reason a player released on account of a domestic violence arrest should be allowed to find a spot with a new team before completing the aforementioned full legal process, investigation and discipline. None."[34] She went on to express her belief that change will only be made when fans, commentators, and ultimately the players within the league start demanding that NFL players be held accountable for their actions.

Reuben Foster was just one of many players who was not expelled from the NFL after his second domestic violence offense, despite the league's stated policy.

Professional athletes are not the only ones committing violent crimes against women. The statistics for crimes such as sexual assault have reached alarming rates on college campuses as well. Author and teacher Jeff Benedict published the first national study of sexual assault and athletes in the 1990s. He discovered that male athletes make up about 3.3 percent of collegiate populations, yet they represent 19 percent of sexual assault perpetrators.

A number of different writers have addressed the question about why athletes commit such crimes. Journalist Mike Imrem, for instance, questioned whether the physical and often violent nature of an athlete's training is responsible. He wrote, "Does the nature of their training translate into abusing women? Athletes are conditioned to be physical, to increase their power, to be aggressive, to be unyielding, to confront challenges, to defy opposition, most of all to win, win, win."[35] When they are taught to dominate and intimidate opponents on the playing field, they may view dating as just another field for them to dominate.

A LEARNED BEHAVIOR

"There must then be something that keeps the football players' violent crime rate as high as it is for other males, and that something is a job in which violence is learned, rehearsed and drilled all day."

—Jeffrey Kluger, writer and editor for *TIME* magazine

Some people believe athletes are no more likely than the general public to commit violent crimes; these people hold the view that an athlete's actions are simply more public, so more people hear about them. However, statistics show that this claim is untrue. In 2014, when the public first began to pay more attention to this issue, statistics website FiveThirtyEight analyzed the rate of NFL convictions compared to that of the general public. It found that NFL players were far more likely than the average person in their income bracket to be arrested for domestic violence. Income is an important factor because statistically, as income rises, rates of domestic violence drop. This is due partially to the fact that people with high incomes live in safer neighborhoods, but it may also be partially due to the fact that people with more money get more respect from police and therefore sometimes find it easier to avoid arrest. The fact that so many rich NFL players are arrested for domestic abuse is, therefore, very significant.

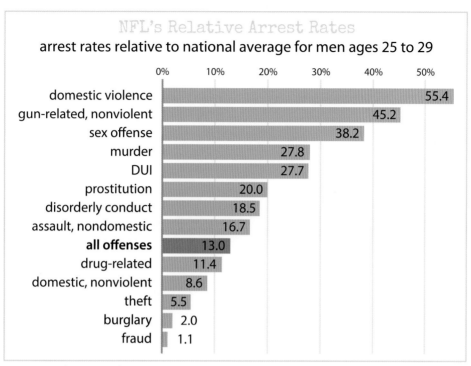

NFL's Relative Arrest Rates

arrest rates relative to national average for men ages 25 to 29

domestic violence	55.4
gun-related, nonviolent	45.2
sex offense	38.2
murder	27.8
DUI	27.7
prostitution	20.0
disorderly conduct	18.5
assault, nondomestic	16.7
all offenses	13.0
drug-related	11.4
domestic, nonviolent	8.6
theft	5.5
burglary	2.0
fraud	1.1

NFL players are disproportionately likely to be arrested for domestic violence, as this information from FiveThirtyEight shows.

Above the Rules?

Sadly, women who accuse athletes—whether in a professional league or on a college team—of a violent act sometimes find that their claims are challenged and their attackers escape punishment of any kind. Reporter Connie Chung explained, "Violence against women is a serious problem on college campuses, and victims who come forward sometimes find themselves fighting the school as well as their attacker."[36]

Two incidents that took place in 1994 clearly illustrate the mentality that prevails on some college campuses. A woman named Kathy Redmond was allegedly raped by a University of Nebraska football star and reported the incident to police as well as to the university. Redmond, in an interview with Chung, reported that she doubted anything would be done, saying,

> [The victim] gets a real feeling of isolation because they think the fans and coaches and management feel that it's a personal attack

against them ... so when you level a charge against an athlete, then all of a sudden you're not battling the athlete, you're battling a whole mindset, you're battling fans, you're battling coaches, you're battling sports management.[37]

Redmond eventually sued the university and received a cash award; the coach also later apologized. The player in question, however, was never disciplined or charged with a crime.

College sports teams can generate a lot of money for their school. This sometimes causes school officials to put pressure on people—particularly women—to stay silent when they accuse a student-athlete of a crime.

Christy Brzonkala was also allegedly raped; she was assaulted by a group of football players from Virginia Tech University. She went to the Virginia Tech coach and reported the rape. The coach's response was typical of the attitude found at some universities: "You know, I'm sorry this happened, but we need to protect our players."[38] The only punishment handed out was that one of the perpetrators had to attend a one-hour educational session. There were no criminal charges filed and no suspensions from the team.

The Danger of CTE

Football players are not the only athletes to be charged with domestic violence. Basketball players, figure skaters, baseball players, NASCAR drivers, wrestlers, boxers, and more have had domestic violence charges leveled against them. However, football players have by far been accused the most. This is mainly due, in two separate ways, to the fact that playing football involves more hands-on action than other sports do. First, this makes violence a learned activity for football players; second, it contributes to more football players getting repeated concussions than athletes in most other sports.

When someone gets repeated concussions—especially if they are put back in the action before their brain has fully recovered, as the NFL has been known to do—they are at risk for developing chronic traumatic encephalopathy (CTE). This is a disease in which the brain slowly but progressively deteriorates, similar to Alzheimer's disease or other forms of dementia, and it has been discovered in 79 percent of former NFL players. The symptoms of CTE include memory loss, behavioral changes, and increased aggression. A link has been made between CTE and violent behavior, including domestic violence and suicide, causing many people to urge the NFL to rework its concussion guidelines and make better efforts to protect its players from head injuries.

Some people believe the NFL has a financial incentive to deny that a link between playing football and developing CTE has been proven and should be used to change policies in the sport. These people point out that it was not until 2016 that the league even admitted the link between playing football and the development of CTE existed.

More research is necessary to reach a definitive conclusion. However, many people believe things need to change to make the NFL safer for players and for others who must deal with the consequences of living with CTE.

Experts say that this failure to punish athletes sends the wrong kind of message to everyone involved. Researcher Andrew SkinnerLopata wrote that athletes develop several inaccurate beliefs this way: "First, that the athletes and the team are all that matters … Second, that male violence against women is acceptable. Third, the bigger star you are, the more you can get away with. Finally, that the athletes really make the rules and that the coaches just try to do damage control. Essentially the message is … boys will be boys."[39]

Feinstein agrees; he stated that because athletes are often looked up to in modern society, the assumption is that the players are above the law. "They are given special privileges in terms of when they go to class," Feinstein said, "and in terms of the meals they eat, in terms of the way they live their lives day in and day out, and they come to believe, to some degree, some of them, that they're above the law in all cases and all situations because they're forgiven their mistakes."[40] Many experts in the field of sports violence believe that this sense of being above the law begins from the moment a young athlete starts displaying an especially good talent for their sport—often as early as high school.

As such, some star athletes believe that they are not subject to the rules that govern others. This comes, in large part, from a society that coddles them and believes they can play a game very well and thus must be protected from the consequences of their own actions. One recent example that received widespread media attention involved Brock Turner, a swimmer at Stanford University who was charged with sexually assaulting an unconscious woman in 2016. Turner faced up to 14 years in jail, but the judge, Aaron Persky, sentenced him to only six months. One of the reasons Persky gave for this sentence was his unwillingness to damage Turner's swimming career and potential future prospects. The light sentence sparked outrage, and in 2018, Persky was recalled from office.

Turner's case is typical of many sexual assault cases; very few men who are accused of rape or sexual assault ever serve jail time. This is especially true not only for athletes, but for other rich, powerful men in general, including movie stars and politicians. Domestic violence experts say that the main reason men abuse women, either physically or sexually, is out of a sense of entitlement. They believe they deserve to get whatever they want, and this belief has been reinforced through various messages over the course of their life—from friends, parents, coaches, the media, and more.

"BAD FOR SOCIETY"

"A survey revealed seventy-six percent of United States adults and eighty-two percent of teens think that it is 'bad for society' to allow athletes to continue their sports career when convicted of a violent crime."

–Bethany P. Withers, lawyer and former editor of the *Harvard Journal of Sports and Entertainment Law*

The way athletes are treated contributes to this sense of entitlement. The general public perceives most athletes as heroes. Their stardom and hero status seem to protect these athletes from official reprimands and punishment. Because the athletes are viewed by the community with awe and fascination, sometimes fans, sports administrators, and officials are willing to overlook actions that might otherwise be condemned. Melvin C. Ray, professor of sociology at Mississippi State University, explained, "Athletes are put on a pedestal. They are given almost free rein to do what they want as long as their teams are in the Top 20."[41] The general public is frequently willing to overlook violence against women—even more so when demanding action might damage their favorite team's chance at winning a championship. The way to address this, many say, is to change society's attitude—a long and difficult, but necessary, process.

CHAPTER 4

Spectator Violence

The prevalence of off-field violence is a continuing problem in sports. However, sometimes athletes are not the only ones acting violent at a game. Violence committed by nonathletes, such as spectators, parents, and coaches, is also a serious and growing concern. Fans have been known to engage in violent acts against athletes, other fans, coaches, and referees. In numerous incidents, spectator violence has also escalated into riots in the stands and around athletic arenas. Parents of young athletes have also committed many acts of violence, as have coaches at all levels of various sports.

Most fans enjoy games without becoming violent. However, some start fights, especially if they have been drinking alcohol or have anger issues.

Soccer Hooligans

Soccer is a massively popular sport with fanatically devoted followers, especially outside of the United States, where the sport is called football. One of the most extreme forms of spectator violence has been occurring with increasing frequency since the early 1960s. Called hooliganism, this form of spectator violence is common at international soccer matches. The term hooliganism was first used by English security forces to describe the violence that was happening at soccer games in that country. This generally takes the form of large-scale riots among fans of opposing teams, who are viewed as literal enemy combatants. Sometimes property damage is done as well.

Soccer is unique among sports today in that it is the only sport where the violence spectators engage in is often worse than what the players do. On-field violence is minimal and typically exaggerated by players with the intention of drawing penalties. International soccer attracts tremendous crowds around the world; it is not unusual for as many as 200,000 people to attend big soccer matches. Soccer fans take their teams and the games very seriously, and the threat of violence is frequently present. According to Jamieson and Orr, "Hooligans often travel to the opposing teams' city to vandalize their opponents' town. The Hooligans representing each team ... square off and fight their battles ... What started as a battle of fists sometimes has become a battle of weapons."[42]

The reason for hooliganism has been partially explained by the fact that soccer teams in Great Britain and other European countries are community based. As a community develops strong emotional bonds with its soccer team, the town often takes losses as personal defeats. This leads to great tension between communities that sometimes bubbles over as riots and other violence at soccer games. Violence can occur at any time—before, during, or after a game. Fights often erupt in bars and neighborhoods the night before a big match.

In contrast to what is sometimes portrayed in films and TV shows, bar fights between fans are not fun, exciting free-for-alls; death statistics as a result of hooliganism can be staggering. In

1995, for example, 39 people were killed and more than 400 were injured in a riot that occurred at a match between a British and an Italian team in Belgium. In 2013, spectators at an event in Brazil stormed the field after a referee stabbed a player to death. The rioters stoned the referee to death and beheaded him. Some fans have also attacked and murdered players who have caused their team to lose an important game. According to Dr. Steve Frosdick, who has studied soccer hooliganism extensively, "From the 1960s to the 1980s, we [saw] a move from spontaneous incidents of soccer-related disorder in the U.K. to organized viciousness."[43] Frosdick and other experts believe soccer rivalries are so intense because they heighten existing political tensions, meaning that solving the issue may be less simple than organizers previously thought. Moderate measures, such as restricting fans' access to alcohol and instituting segregated seating so opposing fans are not as close to each other, have not had the hoped-for results. Even the most extreme tactic—completely banning fans from coming to the stadium—has not worked, because fans tend to simply go to bars to watch the match and start fights there.

"Hooliganism" carries the broad definition of rowdy or violent behavior, but it is almost exclusively applied to violent soccer fans.

GROUPTHINK AT SPORTING EVENTS

"They [individual fans] no longer think as individuals. No one feels personally responsible as long as he or she is doing what everyone else is doing."

–Delia S. Saenz, a psychology professor at the University of Notre Dame

Violence in the Stands

Hooliganism is a term that is almost exclusively restricted to soccer, but soccer fans are by no means the only ones who get rowdy. Spectators enjoy seeing hits in football, violent checks in hockey, and blocked shots in basketball. Cheers erupt when fights break out. Fans enjoy on-field violence. At times, they also become violent themselves. This is true in nearly every sport that is played around the world. Spectator violence can take many forms: celebratory riots, property destruction, fights among opposing fans, throwing objects on the field of play, violent confrontations with players and officials, and drunken brawls. This violence is, of course, not just a modern behavior. According to writers Robert M. Gorman and David Weeks, "As long as there have been spectator sports—even as far back as ancient Rome—there has been violence, and sometimes death, in the stands."[44]

The sports world has witnessed thousands of incidents in the last 100 years that involved fan violence. In baseball, one of the worst examples took place in Cleveland, Ohio, in 1974. In what became known as the "beer night brawl," hundreds of Cleveland Indians baseball fans rushed the field and started beating up the opposing Texas Rangers players during the ninth inning of the game. Several players and one umpire were injured in the ensuing brawl.

Oakland Raiders fans are often easily recognizable by their wild costumes and face paint. They have also gained a reputation for being violent.

The biggest eruption of fan violence in boxing occurred on July 4, 1910, after the first black heavyweight champion, Jack Johnson, had beaten Jim Jeffries, who was known as the White Hope. Racial violence erupted all over the United States following the fight. U.S. Marines had to be called to Norfolk, Virginia, to restore order, while in Keystone, West Virginia, a group of armed black men took over the town. In the days after the fight, as many as 26 people died as a result of violence, more than 250 were injured, and more than 5,000 people were arrested.

Professional football games can also turn ugly when fans get upset. The *Cincinnati Post* reported in 2001, "Standing near midfield, players and officials watched as enraged [Cleveland] Browns fans rained plastic beer bottles, cups, and debris down on them."[45] Members of the opposing team, the Jacksonville Jaguars, ran from the violence; one Jaguars player reported that it was like dodging bullets. The game was stopped for 30 minutes with 48 seconds left. Thousands of bottles needed to be collected from the field before play could resume.

Violence among spectators is also common in collegiate athletics, where some of the most destructive crowd behavior occurs during victory celebrations. Rather than angry fans destructively lashing out, these are wild—often alcohol-fueled—celebrations that get out of hand. After the University of Minnesota won the collegiate hockey championship in 2002, for instance, violence broke out; seven Minnesota students were arrested after police sent 100 officers and 25 firefighters to restore order and put out fires. A similar incident occurred that same year after Ohio State defeated its archrival, the University of Michigan, to advance to the college football championship game. Fans in downtown Columbus rioted; cars were overturned and burned. Police in riot gear used tear gas to disperse the crowd.

The Richard Riot

One of the worst incidents of spectator violence erupted on March 17, 1955, when ice hockey superstar Maurice Richard, or "the Rocket," of the Montreal Canadiens was suspended following an incident on the ice. In addition to slashing an opponent, he also accidentally punched an official. Richard was ejected from the game and suspended from the upcoming Stanley Cup playoffs by NHL commissioner Clarence Campbell.

Montreal fans were infuriated by Campbell's decision, so they gathered outside the arena before his arrival the following evening to protest, yelling insults and waving signs. Later, during the game, a fan punched Campbell in the jaw; others threw programs, eggs, shoes, and other items at him. During one of the intermissions, a smoke bomb exploded inside the arena, and a gunshot was heard. Rushing to restore order, police used tear gas and evacuated the arena. In the panic that followed, thousands of fans stampeded into the Montreal streets, where they overturned and burned cars, looted stores, tore down trolley lines, and fought with police for seven hours. More than 60 people were arrested, and the Canadiens were forced to forfeit the game. The next day, Richard went "live on the radio to address the public, successfully appealing to them to maintain order and end the chaos."[1]

1. "The Richard Riot," Canadiens.com, accessed on April 19, 2019. ourhistory.canadiens.com/greatest-moment/The-Richard-Riot.

Fans at football games sometimes throw things, such as beer cans, cups, and water bottles, on the field when they become upset about a play or a call made by an official.

It is not always surprising that people who have been drinking alcohol, surrounded by screaming spectators, and watching violent, physical sports get caught up in the moment and act out. However, while less common, violence can break out during non-contact sports as well. In some instances, people who are protesting against certain actions use unrelated sporting events as their protest site because they know it will give their protest greater coverage. For example, the Tour de France has been a frequent target, simply because protestors know that interrupting the race is a good way for them to get attention. This can be dangerous for the athletes; in 2018, several competitors had to stop racing when they rode into a cloud of tear gas that was intended to disperse protestors who were trying to block the racecourse with bales of hay. In another incident, colored smoke from a flare blocked the racers' view of the course, causing one of the competitors to fall off his bike. As a result, he lost the race and fractured a vertebra in his spine.

Many protestors of the Tour de France are sheep farmers who are angry about the French government's reintroduction of bears—who have begun killing the sheep, causing the farmers to lose income—to the nearby mountains. Protests at this event have been going on for years; according to the *New York Times*, one of the most famous incidents "occurred in 1984 when Bernard Hinault, a five-time winner of the Tour, punched a shipyard worker who was part of a protest over [work] layoffs that stopped the early-season Paris-Nice race."[46]

What Causes Fan Violence?

Fans who identify with and cheer for their teams can easily lose their focus and behave in ways that they otherwise would not. Experts believe there are many reasons why this may happen. In 2018, after fans in Philadelphia, Pennsylvania, rioted when the Philadelphia Eagles won the Super Bowl, the *Washington Post* published an article discussing the factors that contribute to such riots. According to the article's authors, William Wan and Amy Ellis Nutt, "Researchers attribute violent behavior to a heady mixture of factors: intense fan identification with a team, behavioral changes when people become part of a mob, and strong psychological and physiological [mental and physical] responses when your team wins or loses."[47]

In the United States, experts have found that riots most frequently occur when a team wins rather than when they lose, and the violence tends to be aimed at property rather than at other people—in contrast to hooliganism, where the aim is often to hurt people who support the opposing team. Furthermore, American riots generally happen after a high-stakes game, such as the Super Bowl or an important playoff game.

An important factor in sports riots is the need people have to belong to a group that is similar to them. Daniel Wann, a psychology professor at Murray State University, conducted studies with college students and "found that fans who identify strongly with a team often are less likely to feel lonely or alienated and have higher self-esteem."[48] People who may have nothing else in common can bond over a shared love of a sports team. Because of this, the team starts to be seen as an extension of the person themselves. In studies conducted in the 1990s, social psychologist Edward Hirt found that college basketball fans who saw their team win a game experienced a boost in self-confidence; they "believed they could do much better on

TRYING TO IDENTIFY WITH THE ATHLETES

"[Rioting fans] can't throw a football 60 yards like a quarterback can, but they can throw a rock through the window or pull down a light pole ... To them, it becomes their feat of strength and skill."

—Jerry Lewis, Kent State University sociologist and expert on fan violence

seemingly unrelated tasks, such as solving anagrams [word puzzles] or shooting darts. Those who saw their team lose thought they would do worse."[49] People also experience other changes, such as an increase or decrease in certain brain chemicals.

In addition, there is the issue of what has been called "mob mentality." Numerous studies have shown that people behave differently in a crowd than they might when they are alone.

Winning or losing an important game can lead to riots and massive destruction of property.

People tend to believe they are anonymous, or unidentifiable. They think less about consequences, such as being arrested, when they are one of 500 vandals than when they are doing it alone. Many fans also drink alcohol while watching a sports game, which increases their tendency to make poor choices.

Parents Misbehaving

Another source of sports violence involves parents of youth athletes. Many of today's parents are much more involved in their children's lives than past generations were. This includes sports. Many encourage their children to play a wide variety of sports and then support them and cheer for their success. These parents are normally able to behave appropriately at sporting events, understanding that they are watching children playing a game and not allowing their feelings and emotions to get out of control.

Other parents, however, sometimes behave in an inappropriate and violent manner. *Washington Post* reporter Heather A. Dinich explained, "From Little League to the big leagues and at all level of youth sports in between … more and more parents are crossing the line between being good-natured supporters and overbearing, greedy, and even violent participants in their children's athletic careers."[50]

Experts offer many reasons for such behavior. In some cases, especially in those involving exceptionally talented child athletes, the prospect of fame and fortune for their children makes parents lose their sense of perspective on the sidelines. In other cases, parents see their children's victory or defeat in a sporting event as a direct reflection on them. They get so caught up in the need to see their child win that they fail to remember what is appropriate. This lack of self-control can cause a parent to become verbally abusive toward their child, yelling insults at them from the sidelines if they feel they are not playing well enough. A third reason for this type of violence may be the large amounts of money wealthy parents often spend on their child's sports training, such as lessons with private coaches. These parents may expect to see professional-level playing from their child in return for their financial investment.

One extreme example of parental violence occurred in 2000 in Massachusetts during a hockey practice. Thomas Junta faced manslaughter charges for allegedly beating another parent to death in a dispute over rough play. Junta yelled at and scolded his son for having failed to stick up for himself when another boy pushed him around. Another parent, who was shocked by this behavior and suggested that Junta settle down a little bit, was punched by the enraged father. Later, after the practice was over, Junta beat the man to death in the lobby of the rink in front of the children and other parents. This was believed to be the first documented instance of a fatality involving parental violence at a sporting event in the United States. Junta was later convicted of voluntary manslaughter.

Unfortunately, Junta is not the only parent to behave violently at a child's sporting event. In a survey done by *SportingKid* magazine in 2005, researchers questioned more than 3,000 parents, coaches, administrators, and players about parental violence. The survey showed that 84 percent of those questioned had witnessed parents acting in a violent manner at youth sporting events. Some people believe the incidence of parental sports rage is on the rise, but others believe it is simply more highly publicized since the Junta incident.

Sometimes parents get violent with the players in spite of the fact that they are children. In one example, a soccer father punched a 14-year-old boy in the face because he believed the player had pushed his son around. A possible explanation for this type of behavior involves a parent's protective instincts. Nobody wants to see their child hurt or harassed, and the urge to step in is very strong when these types of behaviors are perceived, regardless of whether or not it is justified. However, the majority of parents can control this urge in situations where it is clear their child is not in any real danger.

It can be very difficult and frustrating for a child to deal with a parent's bad behavior at sporting events. Some possible tactics to decrease this behavior include:

• reminding their parent that sanctioned violence is part of the game and generally does not lead to severe injury

- asking a poorly-behaved parent not to come to games anymore
- asking another adult, such as the coach, to speak to the parent about their behavior
- explaining that it is upsetting or distracting to them to hear their parent yell at them from the sidelines

Parents who resort to extreme violence may be dangerous, and a child's safety should always come first. If someone feels too scared to confront their parent, they should tell another adult who can help keep them safe.

Some parents get upset at sporting events and behave in inappropriate or violent ways.

Other parents and youth players are sometimes the target of parental rage and violence, but more often, parents behave violently toward the officials, yelling or becoming physically violent when the umpire or referee makes a call the parent does not agree with. The National Association of Sports Officials reported in 2018 that more than 70 percent of new referees in all sports quit within three years due to the abuse they receive from parents and coaches. In one incident that occurred in 2018, a parent body-slammed a referee at a youth football game after his son confronted the referee about a call he disagreed with. The father's actions resulted in the entire team being banned from the youth league. Parental violence aimed at referees has become so severe that it has actually resulted in a shortage of referees for youth games, the *New York Times* reported in 2018. No one wants to volunteer for a job where they might end up being attacked, so fewer people than ever before are willing to be referees. This has led to many games being canceled, which means there is less opportunity for young adults to play sports.

In an effort to address this issue, some referees have taken matters into their own hands. Youth soccer referee Brian Barlow of Oklahoma started a Facebook page on which he posts videos of parents behaving badly at games; he said it has made others think twice about behaving the same way out of fear of looking bad and of ending up on the website themselves. Barlow also started a program called Stop Tormenting Officials Permanently (STOP) that hands out signs to be displayed at youth sporting events. These signs carry slogans reminding parents that violent behavior directed at referees will not be tolerated.

PASSING THE BLAME

"If you have your choice to either say my team [stinks] or the refs [stink], which is going to make you feel better?"

–Daniel Wann, professor of psychology at Murray State University, on how personal identification with a team can lead to aggression against referees

This type of parental violence wrongly teaches children—especially those who are playing a physical sport—that it is acceptable to get physical with the referees. In a 2018 incident that an official described as "sickening,"[51] a basketball tournament turned into a brawl involving players and multiple referees after a referee and a player had a verbal disagreement on the court. Howard Martin, the coach of the team that was involved in the fight, expressed disappointment in the way his players behaved, saying, "They're all teenage boys. One guy came to the aid of another guy, which he shouldn't have. He should have let us handle it."[52] Violence against referees—even to the point of death threats—is also not uncommon in the professional leagues.

The most common targets of parental rage and aggression are the referees and umpires officiating children's games.

Coaches as Role Models

In addition to parents and spectators, coaches at all levels of sports can also be guilty of violent acts. This can have tragic consequences, as players and fans often take their behavioral cues from their team's coach. Bob Marshaus of Clinton, Maryland, is a veteran basketball referee and, in 2000, was commissioner of the Maryland Basketball Officials Association. He stated, "I'm a firm believer that everything stems from the coach. If the coach yells at an official, he's like a cheerleader. Fans see that, and they start screaming at officials."[53]

Coaches at all levels of a sport can exhibit bad behavior. For example, in 2015, the *Dallas News* reported that a former assistant coach at John Jay High School in San Antonio, Texas, was accused of telling two of his football players to assault the referee. The coach denied the accusation but resigned from his coaching position. He pled guilty to avoid jail time; instead, he was put on probation for 18 months; ordered to pay a fine and a restitution, or apology, payment to the referee; and ordered to perform 120 hours of community service and attend anger management classes.

In some cases, the coach is encouraged by athletic directors to be hot-tempered and violent if the directors feel it will make for good television and increase the visibility of the program. Bobby Knight, a former college basketball coach, is the most notorious example of this. Considered a brilliant coach who led his teams to an amazing 902 victories and three NCAA basketball championships, Knight was, sadly, better known for his antics on and off the court. According to ESPN, "He was a brilliant coach, but he was also a raging, foul-mouthed bully who'd made headlines for punching a player, fighting a cop, throwing a fan into a trash can, tossing a chair onto the court in the middle of a game."[54]

Some coaches are also guilty of abusing their own players. In youth sports, this might involve forcing the best players to stay in for most of the game, allowing them to exhaust themselves and taking away other players' chance to participate. Some coaches get angry and yell at their players for making mistakes or losing games; some even physically abuse their players. In one example, Rutgers coach Mike Rice was fired by the school in 2013 after video surfaced of Rice "pushing his players, tossing them by the jersey, firing basketballs at their bodies and heads, and ... verbally assaulting his players."[55]

At the college and professional levels, where the stakes for winning are higher, coaches are frequently accused of forcing injured athletes to play instead of resting. Football at all levels

Bobby Knight was considered a brilliant college basketball coach, but his success often came at the expense of others' physical and mental health.

is notorious for intense training sessions. Coaches require strenuous twice-a-day practices in all weather. It is hard enough to engage in vigorous exercise in summer heat; it becomes infinitely more difficult when someone is also wearing several pounds of restrictive padding and equipment. Paul "Bear" Bryant, longtime winning coach at the University of Alabama, was well-known for his aggressive practices. Bryant's goal was to produce tough football players who could endure the worst physical strain, and he showed no mercy on the practice field. *Sports Illustrated* reporter Thomas Lake wrote, "Players who collapsed from heat exhaustion had to crawl to the sideline or be dragged off by student assistants. When a boy fell face-first to the ground from heatstroke, Bryant kicked his fallen body."[56]

Some coaches defend their practices by saying they are "building character" and "turning boys into men." In their view, if the players can handle being pushed like this during practice, they can handle anything that might happen during a game. Players—especially at the high school and college levels—are so determined to prove their dedication and so desperate to belong to the team that they frequently allow themselves to be pushed far past the point of physical discomfort and into dangerous territory. Some sports experts believe hard practices are acceptable as long as the players are monitored for problems throughout the experience, as student-athletes are often not aware enough of their own bodies to understand the danger they may be putting themselves in. Other sociologists and sports experts argue, however, that such coaching behavior is not only careless but violent and abusive, as well as being extremely dangerous for players of all ages.

Sports have become associated with many kinds of violence: sanctioned and unsanctioned violence between players, off-the-field violence, and violent acts committed by spectators, parents, and coaches. Many sociologists, psychologists, and other sports experts are determinedly trying to find ways to prevent such acts.

CHAPTER 5

How Can Violence in Sports Be Prevented?

Regardless of whether the amount of sports violence is increasing or is simply covered in the news more frequently, the fact remains that violence in sports is a problem. Experts have studied this issue for years to try to determine the best way to reduce the number of violent incidents; however, since there are multiple factors that contribute to it, there is no one single solution.

Programs to End Violence at Youth Sporting Events

There have been some steps taken in youth sports to reduce and ultimately prevent violence. In Jupiter, Florida, for instance, Jeff Leslie, president of the Jupiter Tequesta Athletic Association, took action to force parents to curb their acts of violence. The Jupiter Association, in fact, became the first youth sports organization to require parents to attend classes in sportsmanship. While in class, parents are asked to sign a code of ethics promising to promote fair play and control any violent tendencies. If the parents refuse to attend the class or sign the code, their children are not allowed to participate in any sporting activities. Such organizations believe that any change in attitude must start with the parents. Children take their behavioral cues from their parents, and if their parents exhibit good sportsmanship and morality, the children will generally do the same.

In addition to offering sportsmanship classes, some sociologists and psychologists believe athletic leagues should also have "zero tolerance" policies. According to these policies, if parents misbehave, their child would be suspended from play; for second or third incidents, their child would be removed from the team. While some believe it is unfair to punish a child for the actions of their parents, others note that the parents' bad behavior comes from seeing the child as an extension of themselves, making this the most effective way to stop parents from harming others either directly or indirectly. In addition, some leagues are beginning to fine abusive or violent parents. If parents fail to pay the fine, their children are not allowed to play.

Some people believe sportsmanship classes should be required for parents whose children want to play an organized sport.

Not all youth organizations or parents believe that such steps are necessary. In some cases, the leagues rely on the referees and other officials to pinpoint problematic parents and deal with them in an appropriate manner. Parents who habitually cause problems can also be reported to the youth organization. It is then up to the organization to take steps with these individuals to curb violent behavior. These leagues try not to penalize the athletes for the behavior of their parents.

It is also absolutely essential, some sociologists say, that players are educated from the earliest possible age about what is and is not acceptable in athletics. If adults start educating athletes from a young age and instilling good sportsmanship and positive morals in them from the beginning of their athletic careers, these traits will be more likely to stick with them as they advance to higher levels of competition.

PARENTS EXPECT TOO MUCH

"When I got into officiating I looked forward to doing the youth games; I didn't know that was where most of the trouble was ... The parents are all like, 'My kid is going to get that scholarship and be the next LeBron James.' When something isn't going right with that plan, the blame has to go somewhere, and often it's the referee."

–Mary DeLaat, Milwaukee basketball referee who quit in 2014 due to violence and threats aimed at her

Another program dedicated to ending youth sports violence by reintroducing sportsmanship to athletics is the Positive Coaching Alliance, an organization that conducts live and online workshops for coaches, parents, and youth sports groups. Jim Thompson, the founder and executive director, explained that one of the methods the alliance uses is starting conversations about controversial issues in sports and violent incidents that are played on television. Thompson called such incidents "teachable moments," explaining that when parents see violence happening while they are watching a sporting event with their children, they can take that opportunity to explain why it is uncalled for.

Another step many youth leagues have taken is instituting a code of ethics that coaches must sign. These codes, according to the National Alliance for Youth Sports, emphasize that coaches should place the emotional and physical wellbeing of their players ahead of any personal desire to win. Some sports psychologists also suggest that any attempt by the coach to encourage young athletes to perform violent acts should be penalized and, if necessary, that coach should be removed from their position. Experts also believe that leagues should keep a close eye on their coaches; those who run aggressive and abusive practices, they feel, should be closely watched and should face real consequences, such as suspension or firing, if they do things that harm the players either mentally or physically. Experts agree that coaches should treat each player as an individual, lead by example, display fair play and sportsmanship at all times, and provide a safe playing situation for their players.

Some sports fans, however, argue that in many instances, especially at the high school and collegiate levels, coaches are simply trying to deliver what they have been paid to create—winning teams. At the college level and above, in particular, coaches are at risk of being fired for having a losing record. School administrators know that a winning coach will bring in scholarship money and more financing for their athletic programs. This makes many administrators willing to look the other way when complaints are made about an abusive or aggressive coach. Collegiate athletes also tend to tolerate such abuse if they are part of a winning team. It has, for instance, been well

With a record-setting number of wins, Gregg Popovich, head coach of the San Antonio Spurs, has shown that a coach who encourages players can succeed even better than one who abuses them.

documented by sports experts that Bobby Knight bullied his players and sometimes treated them in an abusive way. Even so, most of his former players admire and respect the coach and claim that he taught them well. Some people see this as evidence of a false belief that is common in society: Extreme measures are needed to get extraordinary results. This attitude can be seen in areas besides sports; for example, Steve Jobs, the CEO of Apple, was well-known for being harsh with his employees. He commonly yelled at them and bullied them, but some people still believe his actions were justified because of the innovative products Apple has put out.

Do Penalties Need to Be More Severe?

At the professional and collegiate level, where competition gets more intense, many people believe that players who commit acts of violence on the field are not facing the consequences of their actions. People who hold this view say that the traditional punishments for violent acts, such as small fines and short suspensions, have not been harsh enough to stop players from doing these things again in the future. Sports stars who make millions of dollars a year are not concerned about fines that rarely exceed a few thousand dollars. Many professional sports leagues have begun to implement changes, although most have been criticized for doing so too slowly.

When new NFL commissioner Roger Goodell took over for former commissioner Paul Tagliabue in late 2006, the punishment for violent hits began to change. In September 2008, Goodell announced a new, tougher policy, and wrote in a letter to players, "Football is a tough game and we need to do everything possible to protect all players … from unnecessary injury caused by illegal and dangerous hits … Any conduct that unnecessarily risks the safety of other players has no role in the game of football and will be disciplined at increased levels on a first offense."[57]

Goodell began to punish players by suspending them for much longer periods of time than they had been in the past. During these suspensions, professional football players are not paid, so they risk losing a lot more money than they did before.

While some people have applauded these harsher penalties, others—especially players—have complained that there are now too many rules stopping them from playing the game the way they believe it is meant to be played. Some say it is unfair to punish them for things they may have done unintentionally. Others believe that keeping the new penalties in mind will make players think more carefully about what they do on the field.

Some of NFL commissioner Roger Goodell's changes to the league's penalties have been controversial.

In addition to creating harsher penalties, the NFL has outlawed some moves that were previously legal but led to severe injuries. For example, horse-collar tackles—a move in which a player is pulled down to the ground by the back of their jersey—have been made illegal due to how many players suffered spinal injuries because of them. Furthermore, before the start of the 2018 NFL season, a new rule was put in place that allows officials to immediately stop play to review a hit they suspect might have been illegal. Players now face penalties, including immediate ejection from the game, for deliberately hitting players who are considered defenseless. There are 11 postures the NFL considers to be defenseless, or unable to fight off an opponent who is about to run into them, such as a player who is on the ground or who has just completed a throw. The response to this rule throughout the league has been mixed, with players arguing that these hits are often unintentional and simply part of the game. Some also complain that the penalties are inconsistently applied.

Another sport that has come under recent inspection for its violence is professional ice hockey. Since the beginning of the 21st century, the NHL has tried to curb some of the more vicious forms of unsanctioned violence seen on the ice, particularly hits to the head. As with football, CTE is a serious risk for hockey players—a fact the NHL has only recently accepted. The issue gained increased attention following several blindside hits, or hits coming from an unseen attacker, on star players. For example, on March 7, 2010, Pittsburgh Penguins player Matt Cooke came in from behind, raised his shoulder, and hit Boston Bruins center Marc Savard in the head. No penalty was called, nor was Cooke suspended. Savard ended up with a concussion that kept him out for two months.

That hit and several others led to a meeting of hockey general managers in March 2010 to discuss concussions, head hits, and blind shots. The managers voted to ban blindside hits to the head, defining such hits as any play where a player's head is targeted by another player coming from the first player's blind side. NHL commissioner Gary Bettman stated, "We believe this is the right thing to do for the game and for the safety of our players. The elimination of these types of hits should significantly reduce the number of injuries, including concussions, without adversely affecting the level of physicality in the game."[58] The NHL Players' Association also voted to approve the changes, admitting that such hits had become a concern for players as well. St. Louis Blues' player Jay McClement spoke for many hockey players when he said, "Nobody wants to have the serious injuries in the game, and nobody wants those long-term or career-ending injuries ... I think more than anything it's going to make guys think twice about how they finish their plays."[59]

Although many people believe these actions are good first steps, they are still concerned about the issue of on-the-field violence. Coakley and many other sports experts recommend that to make sure this issue is properly addressed, coaches and team owners as well as players should be fined for player misconduct, as the team officials share much of the responsibility for the style of play that a team participates in.

Preventing Fan Violence

In addition to creating harsher penalties for acts of violence among players, efforts have been made to reduce spectator violence. One of the steps taken has been to control alcohol sales at sporting venues. Many stadiums have instituted alcohol-free zones, while others have banned beer sales toward the ends of games in the hope that fans will have more time to sober up before leaving a sporting event. However, a common practice at NFL games is to tailgate, or hold a pre-game party in the parking lot outside the stadium. Many tailgaters get very drunk before the game even starts, leading the NFL to put new policies in place that allow security to deny someone entry if they seem too drunk. While this has resulted in fewer incidents of violence during the games, the number of incidents in parking lots has risen.

Violence in the stands between strangers and even between friends is a frequent occurrence at sporting events. These experiences range from someone pouring a drink on someone else to someone being insulted or being spit on. Today, many athletic arenas encourage fans to call or text posted phone numbers to report disruptive individuals in the stands. Some stadiums, such as the Brewers' MLB stadium in Milwaukee, Wisconsin, have created zero tolerance policies, throwing fans out as soon as they start trouble. The NFL has also created its own zero tolerance policy where, if someone is thrown out of a game, they are banned from buying tickets to any future games until they pay $250 to take a good behavior test and write a letter to the team whose game they disrupted asking for permission to come to games again. Many stadiums have also increased the number of security guards and police at events.

The presence of police and security guards prohibit fans from streaming onto the field or court after a game—an occurrence that used to be relatively common in professional sports.

Other leagues have different policies; fans who cause multiple disturbances or who are far more disruptive than most others may face bans from future games. For example, in 2019, a fan of the Utah Jazz NBA franchise was permanently banned from all future events at the Jazz arena after officials determined that he had excessively displayed abusive behavior toward Oklahoma City Thunder point guard Russell Westbrook.

Most stadiums and other sports arenas now have metal detectors; fans are also searched before they are allowed to enter stadiums to make sure they are not bringing weapons in. In England, the Football Spectators Act of 1989 was passed to allow courts to punish fans who engage in hooliganism. This can apply to things such as throwing objects on the field or yelling racist slurs, as well as violence or property damage done up to 24 hours after a match. Several amendments to the act have been passed since 2000.

Expecting More from Referees

Many sports experts suggest that closer officiating during athletic events could help reduce violence. In baseball, for instance, when a pitcher intentionally hits a batter, umpires are now acting to punish such incidents. If an umpire believes the pitcher is throwing deliberately at another player, the pitcher is first given a warning. If he continues to throw such pitches, he is ejected from the game and fined—so are opposing pitchers who try to retaliate. While this has not completely eliminated such tactics, many experts feel such ejections and fines are a big step in the right direction.

Dean Smith, former basketball coach of the University of North Carolina Tar Heels, believes that both college and professional basketball could benefit from closer officiating. He said that officials should be instructed by their supervisors to call all fouls to keep games from getting too rough or out of control. In fact, he suggested that the NCAA hire full-time officials for college basketball games. Smith explained, "Such a system would give supervisors control over their officials. If officials didn't call the game the way it was meant to be called, the supervisors could dismiss them."[1] Instead, most of the men and women who work as officials in college basketball have full-time jobs outside the sport. This is true in football as well, where officials are often inconsistent in calling penalties for violent acts. While it is often difficult to separate a sanctioned hit from a cheap shot, referees have been criticized for not calling enough penalties.

1. Dean Smith, John Kilgo, and Sally Jenkins, *A Coach's Life: My 40 Years in College Basketball.* New York, NY: Random House, 1999, p. 278.

Some critics of spectator behavior also assert that the police must become more involved in instances where spectators act in a violent manner. At a certain point, bans are not enough. If someone behaves violently, these critics believe, that person should face legal consequences, just as they would if they were outside of the stadium.

A number of sports experts also agree that athletic administrators at the high school and college level need to improve their relationship with local police, school police, and security forces. Journalist Donald C. Collins explained,

> *Administrators can usually predict problems they'll confront in their gyms in advance. They know or should know which spectators have a history of violence or have scores to settle, and which neighborhoods have rivalries. Armed with that knowledge, they can take steps to minimize the risk of violence as much as possible, such as by using a metal detector ... and by having enough security personnel on site for crowd control.*[60]

Metal detectors have been put in place in many public buildings, including sports arenas, to prevent people from bringing in weapons.

Despite the violence from spectators, some owners are still reluctant to deal with fans who get out of hand in case it affects ticket sales. It can be difficult for owners to balance taking care of their players and fans with maximizing their profits and revenue.

Efforts have also been made to reduce violence against referees. In addition to Brian Barlow's STOP program, which has been gaining widespread interest from youth leagues, other programs have been put into action. In South Carolina, for instance, the state's Youth Soccer Association instituted a policy in 2017 called Silent September. Under this policy, for an entire month, clapping was the only noise allowed; fans were not allowed to yell or cheer. According to Burns Davison, who is in charge of rules and compliance for the association, "It was a resounding success and made for a much more focused environment for learning and for play."[61]

These types of policies are necessary, many say, because of the extreme violence referees are increasingly facing. Barlow and two other referees needed armed police to escort them to their cars after one 2018 game, and his 12-year-old daughter, who referees soccer games for 6-year-olds, also received threats of violence from parents who did not like the calls she made.

When Should the Police Step In?

With the police often helping to reduce spectator violence, some sports experts are questioning whether police should also be involved in on-field acts of violence committed by the athletes. The police and court system, for the most part, have been very reluctant to get involved in incidents of violence on the playing field. The belief was that what happened on the field should be dealt with on the field. Even in cases where players were severely injured by unsanctioned violence, those players were reluctant to testify or press charges against an aggressor. Consent is an important part of charging someone with assault; by agreeing to play a game that involves sanctioned violence, players consent to a certain amount of shoving, tackling, or other roughness, and many serious injuries are the result of accidents that result during the normal course of the game rather than deliberate attempts to hurt someone. The difficulty is in determining where consent for this violence ends.

Law enforcement has sometimes been involved in unsanctioned violence, though. Canada has often been more willing to bring charges against athletes for violence during sporting events than the United States. For example, in 1969, two hockey players faced assault charges after a fight, although the charges were later dropped.

POLICE NEED TO STEP IN

"If the leagues are doing such a good job policing themselves, why does the violence persist?"

–Kris Axtman, writer for the *Christian Science Monitor*

Guilty verdicts became more common in the early 21st century. Boston Bruins defenseman Marty McSorley was charged with assault with a deadly weapon after an on-ice incident on February 21, 2000. McSorley attacked Vancouver Canucks player Donald Brashear with his stick; Brashear was struck in the head and immediately dropped unconscious to the ice, suffering a severe concussion. McSorley was suspended by the NHL for the remaining 23 games of the season as well as the playoffs. It was the harshest penalty ever imposed by the league up to that time. He was also charged with assault by the Vancouver police and faced up to 18 months in jail. McSorley was found guilty of the charges, but instead of going to jail, he was placed on 18 months of probation. Following the conviction, the NHL suspended McSorley for an additional year; he never played another game.

In another hockey incident, Dino Ciccarelli of the Minnesota North Stars was sentenced to one day in jail and fined $1,000 for striking Toronto defenseman Luke Richardson several times in the head with his stick. Prosecution has also happened, rarely, in basketball, but it is almost nonexistent in other sports. According to sportswriter Gerald Eskenazi, "There is a long tradition in organized sports … that they police themselves."[62]

Preventing Violence Off the Field

In addition to questioning whether law enforcement needs to be involved in sports violence, experts also question the efforts being made to curb off-the-field violence committed by athletes. Many sports leagues, for example, are increasingly using counseling, fines, and the threat of suspension to stop players from committing violent crimes. Many critics still believe, however, that professional leagues are not doing enough.

Many colleges and universities are also beginning to take small steps to reduce violence committed by athletes on campus, particularly sexual violence. When a collegiate athlete or other student is charged with sexual assault or rape, a few universities are now beginning to apply academic punishments, such as suspension from school for a period of time or outright expulsion. However, this is part of a wider issue of rape accusations not being taken seriously enough by universities. In addition to being concerned about their athletic programs, schools worry about their reputation and are more likely to try to hide or dismiss accusations than to investigate them. Many advocates are working to change this attitude.

The National Coalition Against Violent Athletes is one organization working to further address the issue of sexual assault on campus by making efforts to ensure that offending athletes are held accountable for their actions. According to experts, awareness of sexual assault in general needs to be discussed further. Sexual assault is a very broad term that encompasses many types of behaviors. Students need to be educated on what can be considered sexual assault, as many of them have a very narrow definition of the term in mind. Communication needs to be improved. These issues should be discussed openly and often, experts stress, rather than swept under the rug. Women have long been educated on how to avoid being sexually assaulted. It is time, many people argue, for society to focus on raising generations of men who do not see these types of behavior as appropriate.

Some sports experts are now suggesting that in order to decrease collegiate sports violence, universities should investigate a high school athlete's criminal past before the school offers them a scholarship. In 2010, *Sports Illustrated* and CBS Sports did a study of high school football recruits to the top 25 college football teams, according to preseason rankings. The survey, published in March 2011, showed that 7 percent of the high school athletes had criminal records; 40 percent of those were for serious offenses such as assault and battery, burglary, and sexual assault.

Many experts believe that an increased emphasis on sportsmanship can help put the fun back into sports.

While some college administrators believe that scholar-ships should never be given to athletes with criminal records, a number of coaches disagree. Writer George Dohrmann explained, "They [the coaches] know that not every kid—or every crime—is the same ... It would lessen the sport's power to change lives."[63] These coaches believe that college sports and the university atmosphere can help athletes find meaning and purpose in life and lead them away from lives of crime. For many student-athletes, their sport is their way out. They may have grown up in difficult neighborhoods and gotten involved in things they should not have been involved in. Not allowing them to attend college due to past indiscretions leaves them in the same situation, with no opportunity for self-improvement.

Violence in sports, both sanctioned and unsanctioned, will remain a point of contention between fans and critics for the foreseeable future. It is nearly impossible to remove all ele-ments of sanctioned violence from a contact sport. However, if appropriate research continues to be done into the causes of unsanctioned violence and changes are made, it should be possible to drastically reduce the tragic incidents that are all too often the result of the "win at all costs" attitude that is so common in today's sports.

If parents and coaches of youth sports can be convinced to start emphasizing sportsmanship from a young age, they may be able to create positive change in the future. Ultimately, no matter what level of competition an athlete is participating in, no matter how much money they are making to compete, and no matter how important winning feels in the moment, they must remember that they are only playing a game.

NOTES

Introduction: Violence Around the World

1. Quoted in Nationwide Children's Hospital, "Prevalence of Sports-Related Violence Increasing," Newswise, January 13, 2006. www.newswise.com/articles/view/517287.

2. Jay Coakley, *Sports in Society: Issues and Controversies.* Boston, MA: McGraw-Hill, 2007, p. 153.

3. Quoted in John H. Kerr, *Rethinking Aggression and Violence in Sport.* London, England: Routledge, 2005, p. 7.

4. Quoted in Viv Saunders, "Sport and 20th Century American Society," *History Review*, vol. 66, March 2010.

5. Saunders, "Sport and 20th Century American Society."

6. Lynn Jamieson and Thomas Orr, *Sport and Violence: A Critical Examination of Sport.* Oxford, England: Butterworth-Heinemann, 2009, p. 1.

Chapter 1: What Is Allowed?

7. Jonathon Hardcastle, "Sports Violence," *Ezine Articles*, September 5, 2006. ezinearticles.com/?Sports-Violence&id=290850.

8. Quoted in Thomas Tutko, *Winning Is Everything and Other American Myths.* New York, NY: MacMillian, 1976, p. 18.

9. "Student-Athletes Unaware of Their Career Ending Injuries," Pro Athlete Law Group, accessed on April 15, 2019. proathletelawgroup.com/student-athletes-unaware-of-their-career-ending-injuries/.

10. "Carlisle: 'I Was Fighting for My Life Out There,'" ESPN, November 27, 2004. www.espn.com/nba/recap?gameId=241119008.

11. Fred Engh, *Why Johnny Hates Sports*. New York, NY: Square One, 2002, p. 16.

12. "UI Study Finds Fewer Fans Watching NASCAR for the Crashes," University of Iowa Office of the Vice President for Research, accessed on April 15, 2019. research.uiowa.edu/ui-study-finds-fewer-fans-watching-nascar-crashes.

13. Steven Kotler, "Are Sports Making Our Children More Violent?," *Psychology Today*, July 14, 2008. www.psychologytoday.com/us/blog/the-playing-field/200807/are-sports-making-our-children-more-violent.

14. Kotler, "Are Sports Making Our Children More Violent?"

Chapter 2: Violence and Competition

15. Kerr, *Rethinking Aggression and Violence in Sport*, p. 61.

16. Quoted in Tutko, *Winning Is Everything and Other American Myths*, p. 4.

17. Quoted in Engh, *Why Johnny Hates Sports*, p. 27.

18. Engh, *Why Johnny Hates Sports*, p. 27.

19. "Sports: When Winning Is the Only Thing, Can Violence Be Far Away?," Canadian Centres for Teaching Peace, accessed on May 8, 2019. www.peace.ca/sports.htm.

20. Larry M. Lance and Charlynn E. Ross, "Views of Violence in American Sports: A Study of College Students," *College Student Journal*, vol. 34, no. 2, June 2000. www.questia.com/library/journal/1G1-131318265/views-of-violence-in-american-sports-a-study-of-college.

21. Jamieson and Orr, *Sport and Violence*, p. 72.

22. Coakley, *Sports in Society*, p. 203.

23. Jeré Longman, "For All the Wrong Reasons, Women's Soccer Is Noticed," *New York Times*, November 10, 2009. www.nytimes.com/2009/11/11/sports/soccer/11violence.html.

24. Quoted in Longman, "For All the Wrong Reasons."

25. Quoted in Longman, "For All the Wrong Reasons."

26. Coakley, *Sports in Society*, p. 202.

27. Quoted in Keith Joseph, "Violence in Sport—An Age-Old Problem Finally Highlighted," St Vincent and the Grenadines Olympic Committee, September 26, 2014. svgnoc.org/blog/violence-in-sport-an-age-old-problem-finally-highlighted/.

28. Quoted in Coakley, *Sports in Society*, p. 207.

29. Kerr, *Rethinking Aggression and Violence in Sport*, p. 85.

Chapter 3: Violence Off the Field

30. Quoted in Tom Jacobs, "Gridiron Violence Off the Field," *Pacific Standard*, last updated May 21, 2018. psmag.com/social-justice/gridiron-violence-off-the-field-4752.

31. Jacobs, "Gridiron Violence."

32. Quoted in "Violence in the Personal Lives of Amateur Athletes," *Morning Edition*, NPR, September 18, 1995.

33. Dayana Sarkisova, "When It Comes to Domestic Violence, Stop Expecting NFL Teams to Do the Right Thing," SBNation, November 28, 2018. www.sbnation.com/2018/11/28/18116222/reuben-foster-nfl-washington-domestic-violence-collective-bargaining-agreement.

34. Sarkisova, "When It Comes to Domestic Violence."

35. Mike Imrem, "Does Violence in Sports Transfer to Homestead?," *Arlington Heights Daily Herald*, July 26, 2002.

36. Connie Chung, "Violent Athletes," *Good Morning America*, March 9, 1998.

37. Quoted in Chung, "Violent Athletes."

38. Quoted in Chung, "Violent Athletes."

39. Andrew SkinnerLopata, "Athletes Can Set Example on Domestic Violence," *Eugene Register-Guard*, March 3, 2010. special.registerguard.com/csp/cms/sites/web/opinion/24515069-47/violence-athletes-women-team-football.csp.

40. Quoted in "Violence in the Personal Lives of Amateur Athletes," *Morning Edition*.

41. Quoted in Jerry Kirshenbaum, "An American Disgrace," *Sports Illustrated*, February 27, 1989. www.si.com/vault/1989/02/27/119471/an-american-disgrace-a-violent-and-unprecedented-lawlessness-has-arisen-among-college-athletes-in-all-parts-of-the-country.

Chapter 4: Spectator Violence

42. Jamieson and Orr, *Sport and Violence*, p. 120.

43. Quoted in Tiffanie Wen, "A Sociological History of Soccer Violence," *The Atlantic*, July 14, 2014. www.theatlantic.com/health/archive/2014/07/a-sociological-history-of-soccer-violence/374396/.

44. Robert M. Gorman and David Weeks, *Death at the Ballpark: A Comprehensive Study of Game-Related Fatalities of Players, Other Personnel and Spectators in Amateur and Professional Baseball: 1862–2007*. Jefferson, NC: McFarland, 2009, p. 146.

45. "Cleveland Fans Turn Violent," *Cincinnati Post*, December 7, 2001.

46. Ian Austen, "The Tour de France Hits a Cloud of Tear Gas and Comes to a Stop," *New York Times*, July 24, 2018. www.nytimes.com/2018/07/24/sports/tour-de-france-tear-gas.html.

47. William Wan and Amy Ellis Nutt, "Why Do Fans Riot After a Win? The Science Behind Philadelphia's Super Bowl Chaos," *Washington Post*, February 5, 2018. www.washingtonpost.com/news/to-your-health/wp/2018/02/05/why-do-fans-riot-after-a-win-the-science-behind-philadelphias-super-bowl-chaos/?utm_term=.8416b3a17813.

48. Wan and Nutt, "Why Do Fans Riot After a Win?"

49. Wan and Nutt, "Why Do Fans Riot After a Win?"

50. Heather A. Dinich, "From Backers to Attackers," *Washington Post*, July 26, 2000. www.washingtonpost.com/archive/sports/2000/07/26/from-backers-to-attackers/57177e5a-6cb9-4cfc-8fca-695447fdbc51/.

51. Quoted in Des Bieler, "'It's Sickening': Players Brawl with Referees During Basketball Tournament," *Washington Post*, July 9, 2018. www.washingtonpost.com/news/early-lead/wp/2018/07/09/its-sickening-players-brawl-with-referees-during-basketball-tournament/.

52. Quoted in Bieler, "'It's Sickening.'"

53. Quoted in Mark Stewart, "Good Sports?," *Insight on the News*, June 19, 2000.

54. Jay Lovinger, ed., *The Gospel According to ESPN: Saints, Saviors, and Sinners*. New York, NY: Hyperion, 2002, p. 80.

55. "Coaches Fired for Alleged Verbal and Physical Abuse of Players," NBC Sports, accessed on April 22, 2019. www.nbcsports.com/coaches-fired-alleged-verbal-and-physical-abuse-players.

56. Thomas Lake, "The Boy Who Died of Football," *Sports Illustrated*, December 6, 2010. www.si.com/vault/2010/12/06/106012866/the-boy-who-died-of-football.

Chapter 5: How Can Violence in Sports Be Prevented?

57. Quoted in "Jets' Smith Suspended One Game, Fined $50k for Hit on Boldin," NFL, last updated July 26, 2012. www.nfl.com/news/story/09000d5d80b3c79c/article/jets-smith-suspended-one-game-fined-50k-for-hit-on-boldin.

58. Quoted in "NHL Players' Union Approves New Head Shot Ban," NHL.com, March 25, 2010. www.nhl.com/news/nhl-players-union-approves-new-head-shot-ban/c-522700.

59. Quoted in Dan O'Neill, "NHL Cracks Down on Hits to the Head," *St. Louis Post-Dispatch*, March 25, 2010. www.stltoday.com/sports/hockey/professional/article_1d349039-1d33-51ce-a19b-95be6598fea3.html.

60. Donald C. Collins, "Gun Violence at Youth Sports Contests: An Ever Present Threat in Urban Areas," MomsTeam, accessed on May 17, 2019. www.momsteam.com/team-of-experts/gun-violence-at-athletic-contests-an-administrators-nightmare.

61. Quoted in Bill Pennington, "Parents Behaving Badly: A Youth Sports Crisis Caught on Video," *New York Times*, July 18, 2018. www.nytimes.com/2018/07/18/sports/referee-parents-abuse-videos.html.

62. Gerald Eskenazi, "Arrest Pro Athletes for On-Field Assaults," *Observer*, November 12, 2015. observer.com/2015/11/arrest-pro-athletes-for-on-the-field-assaults/.

63. George Dohrmann, "Rap Sheets, Recruits, and Repercussions," *Sports Illustrated*, March 7, 2011. www.si.com/vault/2011/03/07/106043456/rap-sheets-recruits-and-repercussions.

DISCUSSION QUESTIONS

Chapter 1: What Is Allowed?

1. How are the lines between sanctioned and unsanctioned violence blurred in different sports?

2. Do you think sanctioned violence is all part of the game, or should it be discouraged?

3. Does violence, either sanctioned or unsanctioned, affect how you feel about playing sports?

Chapter 2: Violence and Competition

1. What factors affect the winning-at-all-costs mindset?

2. Do you think athletes today are less interested in sportsmanship than they used to be? Why or why not?

3. What are some ways players can increase fair play in their sport?

Chapter 3: Violence Off the Field

1. Is there a connection between violence on and off the field?

2. Why do you think people tend to look the other way when athletes are charged with domestic violence or sexual assault?

3. What is entitlement? How can it be addressed?

Chapter 4: Spectator Violence

1. Can you think of a time when you got caught up in crowd mentality and acted in a way you normally wouldn't?

2. What are some ways to deal with parental spectator violence that were not discussed in the book?

3. What type of behavior from a coach would encourage violence? What type of behavior would discourage it?

Chapter 5: How Can Violence in Sports Be Prevented?

1. What steps are professional sports leagues taking to control violence on the field of play? Is it effective?

2. How should you act when you are at a sports game?

3. How can colleges and universities prevent sexual violence?

ORGANIZATIONS TO CONTACT

Josephson Institute

8117 W. Manchester Avenue #830

Playa del Rey, CA 90293

josephsoninstitute.org

twitter.com/Josephson0

www.youtube.com/user/josephsoninstitute

> The Josephson Institute is an organization dedicated to the improvement of ethical standards in society, including in sports.

National Alliance for Youth Sports

2050 Vista Parkway

West Palm Beach, FL 33411

www.nays.org

www.instagram.com/nays_youthsports

twitter.com/NAYS_edu

www.youtube.com/user/nationalalliance4ys

> The National Alliance for Youth Sports is a nonprofit organization that works to provide a safe and positive sports experience for children and teens.

Northeastern University Center for the Study of Sport in Society

360 Huntington Avenue, 42 Belvidere

Boston, MA 02115

www.northeastern.edu/sportinsociety

www.instagram.com/sportinsociety

twitter.com/sportinsociety

> The Northeastern University Center for the Study of Sport in Society is a research facility that studies the impact of sports on society and works to move sports culture away from the idea that winning is everything.

Positive Coaching Alliance
1001 N. Rengstorff Avenue, Suite 100
Mountain View, CA 94043
www.positivecoach.org
twitter.com/PositiveCoachUS
    The Positive Coaching Alliance is an organization that provides
    tools for coaches and parents to enhance youth athletics.

FOR MORE INFORMATION

Books

Asselin, Kristine Carlson. *What You Need to Know About Concussions.* London, England: Raintree, 2016.
> Concussions are a risk in several sports, and studies have shown that they can increase the incidence of violence. This book explains how concussions affect the brain and how they can be prevented.

Bowker, Paul. *Issues in Sports: Violence in Sports.* Minneapolis, MN: ABDO Publishing Company, 2014.
> The author looks at the trend of violence in sports and how it is being addressed.

Brezina, Corona. *Everything You Need to Know About Anger Management.* New York, NY: Rosen YA, 2019.
> For athletes who find themselves committing violent acts, anger management may be a good first step toward changing their behavior.

Roesler, Jill. *Asking Questions About Violence in Popular Culture.* Ann Arbor, MI: Cherry Lake Publishing, 2016.
> When people do not think critically about the violence they see in the media, it can affect the way they behave in everyday life. This book examines how people decide what is too violent to show the public, how those standards have changed over time, and what effects society's increasing tolerance of violence is having on people.

Websites

American Association of Neurological Surgeons: Concussion
www.aans.org/Patients/Neurosurgical-Conditions-and-Treatments/Concussion
> This web page explains the symptoms of a concussion and the link between the NFL and brain trauma.

Canadian Centre for Ethics in Sport
www.cces.ca
> The Canadian Centre for Ethics in Sport is a nonprofit organization dedicated to promoting drug-free sports, fair play, safety, and nonviolence.

KidsHealth: Sportsmanship
kidshealth.org/en/parents/sportsmanship.html
> This web page teaches parents as well as players more about how to be a good sport.

National Coalition Against Violent Athletes
ncava.org
> The National Coalition Against Violent Athletes is an organization dedicated to eliminating violence committed by athletes off the field, particularly sexual violence.

The Spruce: "Spectator Sports Etiquette"
www.thespruce.com/spectator-sports-etiquette-1216647
> This article explains how to be a good spectator at a sporting event.

INDEX

A

Abdul-Jabbar, Kareem, 24
Abrams, Mitch, 39
aggression, 8, 16–17, 27, 30–32, 37–38, 40, 53, 68–69
alcohol, 9, 27, 58, 61–62, 65, 79
Allen, A'Don, 40
Armstrong, Lance, 35
Artest, Ron, 23
Axtman, Kris, 84

B

Barlow, Brian, 68, 83
baseball, 16, 23, 35, 41, 59, 81
basketball, 21–22, 24, 68, 70, 81, 85
beanballs, 23
Benedict, Jeff, 46, 49
Bertuzzi, Todd, 42
Bettman, Gary, 78
blindsiding, 19, 78
boxing, 6, 14, 21, 23, 25, 60
Brown, Larry, 23
Bryant, Paul, 71
Brzonkala, Christy, 52

C

Campbell, Clarence, 61
Chapman, Ray, 41–42
cheap shots, 16–17, 19, 44, 81
chronic traumatic encephalopathy (CTE), 53, 78
Chung, Connie, 51
Ciccarelli, Dino, 85
Clinton, Bill, 8

coaches, 33–34, 36–37, 69–71, 74–76
Coakley, Jay, 7, 38, 40, 79
college sports, 20, 35–37, 59, 51–52, 60–61, 71, 75–76, 81, 86–87
Collins, Donald C., 82
concussions, 19, 21, 23, 42, 53, 78, 84
consent, 83–84
Cooke, Matt, 78
crimes, 19, 23, 28, 46–50, 52, 55, 85, 87

D

DeLaat, Mary, 74
Dinich, Heather A., 65
Dohrmann, George, 87
domestic violence, 27, 47–51, 53, 55
Dorrance, Anson, 39
Doughty, Stanley, 18

E

Ellis Nutt, Amy, 63
endorphins, 32
Engh, Fred, 25, 34
Eskenazi, Gerald, 85
Everett, Kevin, 20

F

fans, 9, 22, 26, 40, 56–61, 63, 65, 79–80, 83
Feinstein, John, 24, 47, 54
figure skating, 33–34

football, 14, 18–20, 27, 29, 46–47, 53, 60, 71, 76, 86
Football Spectators Act of 1989, 80
Foster, Reuben, 48–49
Frosdick, Steve, 58

G

Goodell, Roger, 76–77
Gorman, Robert M., 59
Griffin, Pat, 39

H

Hardcastle, Jonathon, 12
Harding, Tonya, 33–34
Hargrove, Anthony, 20
high school sports, 18–19, 71, 75, 86
Hirt, Edward, 63
hockey, 11, 14–16, 21–22, 26, 38, 40, 42, 61, 66, 78
Holyfield, Evander, 23
hooliganism, 57–59, 63, 80
Houston, Graham, 21
Hunger Games, The (Collins), 13

I

Imrem, Mike, 49
injuries, 10–11, 14, 18–21, 34, 41–42

J

Jamieson, Lynn, 8, 37, 57
Jeffries, Jim, 60
Johnson, Jack, 60
Josephson Institute, 43–44
Junta, Thomas, 66
Jupiter Tequesta Athletic Association, 72

K

Karras, Alex, 17–18

Kelly, Yusef, 21
Kerr, John H., 31–32, 44
Kerrigan, Nancy, 33–34
Kluger, Jeffrey, 50
Knight, Bobby, 70, 76
Knox, Johnny, 20
Kreager, Derek, 28–29, 46–47

L

Lambert, Elizabeth, 38–39
Lance, Larry M., 37
Leslie, Jeff, 72
Lewis, Jerry, 64
Lombardi, Vince, 33
Lundberg, George D., 26

M

Major League Baseball (MLB), 41–42
Marshaus, Bob, 69
May, Brad, 42
Mays, Carl, 41
McSorley, Marty, 84
media, 11, 25, 27–28, 38–39, 47
management, 40
mental illnesses, 32
Miller, Kathleen, 47
mixed martial arts, 14–15
mob mentality, 64
Moore, Steve, 42

N

Naismith, James A., 21–22
NASCAR, 12, 26
Näslund, Markus, 42
National Basketball Association (NBA), 22–24, 40, 46, 80
National Coalition Against Violent Athletes, 85
National Collegiate Athletic Association (NCAA), 18, 21, 70, 81

National Football Association (NFL), 33, 40, 46–51, 53, 76–79
National Hockey League (NHL), 16, 26, 40, 42, 61, 78, 84

O

Orr, Thomas, 8, 37, 57

P

parents, 30, 65–69, 72–74, 83
penalties, 11, 15–16, 19, 22, 38, 42–43, 48, 57, 77–79, 81, 84
performance-enhancing drugs, 9, 35
police, 50–51, 61, 80–84
Positive Coaching Alliance, 74
practices, 30, 71, 75
punishments, 35, 51–52, 55, 76, 85

R

Ray, Melvin C., 55
Redmond, Kathy, 51–52
referees, 16, 67–69, 74, 81, 83
retaliation, 41–43
Rice, Mike, 70
Rice, Ray, 47–48
Richard, Maurice, 61
Richardson, Luke, 85
riots, 57–58, 61, 63–64
roller derby, 38
Rome, 12–13, 59
Ross, Charlynn E., 37
Russell, Gordon W., 8

S

Saenz, Delia S., 59
Sarkisova, Dayana, 47–49
Saunders, Viv, 8
Savard, Marc, 78
sensationalism, 25, 38–39

sexual assault, 23, 49, 54, 85–86
Silent September, 83
SkinnerLopata, Andrew, 54
Smith, Dean, 81
soccer, 38, 57–58
spectator violence, 56–57, 59, 61, 79, 83
sportsmanship, 21, 34, 43–45, 72, 74–75, 86
Stingley, Darryl, 19
Stop Tormenting Officials Permanently (STOP), 68, 83

T

Tagliabue, Paul, 76
Tatum, Jack, 19
Thor: Ragnarok (film), 13
Toffel, Paul, 24
Tomjanovich, Rudy, 24
Tour de France, 35, 62
Turner, Brock, 54
Tyson, Mike, 23

W

Wallace, Ben, 23
Wan, William, 63
Wann, Daniel, 63, 68
warriors, 12, 37–38, 40
Washington, Kermit, 24
Weeks, David, 59
Wilbon, Mike, 15
Withers, Bethany P., 55
wrestling, 6, 29

Y

Yaeger, Don, 46
youth sports, 12, 28, 30, 36, 44, 66, 68, 70, 72, 74, 87

Z

zero tolerance policies, 73, 79

PICTURE CREDITS

Cover Herbert Kratky/Shutterstock.com; p. 6 Nick Potts/PA Images via Getty Images; p. 9 Kevin C. Cox - FIFA/FIFA via Getty Images; p. 13 Frazer Harrison/Getty Images; p. 15 Stefan Holm/Shutterstock.com; p. 20 KJ/Icon SMI/Icon Sport Media via Getty Images; p. 22 Matthew Jacques/Shutterstock.com; p. 25 Dave Sandford/NHLI via Getty Images; p. 29 Aspen Photo/Shutterstock.com; p. 32 sirtravelalot/Shutterstock.com; p. 33 Bettmann/Bettmann/Getty Images; p. 36 Fotokostic/Shutterstock.com; p. 37 SpeedKingz/Shutterstock.com; p. 42 George Rinhart/Corbis via Getty Images; p. 43 Action Sports Photography/Shutterstock.com; p. 48 Andrew Burton/Getty Images; p. 49 Cody Glenn/Icon Sportswire via Getty Images; p. 52 John Jones/Icon Sportswire via Getty Images; p. 56 Gregory Fisher/Icon Sportswire via Getty Images; p. 58 Nicolò Ongaro/NurPhoto via Getty Images; p. 60 Jane Tyska/Digital First Media/The Mercury News via Getty Images; p. 62 David Maxwell/AFP/Getty Images; p. 64 Rick Friedman/Corbis via Getty Images; p. 67 Toshifumi Hotchi/Shutterstock.com; p. 69 Flavio Beltran/Shutterstock.com; p. 70 Jamie Squire/Getty Images; pp. 73, 86 Monkey Business Images/Shutterstock.com; p. 75 Gene Sweeny Jr./Getty Images; p. 77 Andy Lyons/Getty Images; p. 80 Sergey Granev/Shutterstock.com; p. 82 James Chance/Getty Images.

ABOUT THE AUTHOR

Tyler Stevenson is a professional in the health insurance industry. He graduated from the University at Buffalo with a degree in sociology and originally went into banking before making the switch to health insurance. He works in Buffalo, New York, and lives in the City of Tonawanda with his wife and two young daughters.